Donna's #'s
cell 9156-9058
home 2592-9058

Hong Kong

Berlitz Publishing Company, Inc.
Princeton   Mexico City   London   Eschborn   Singapore

Berlitz Trademark Reg. U.S. Patent Office and other countries
Marca Registrada

Text:	Alice Fellows
Editor:	Media Content Marketing, Inc.
Photography:	Jon Davison; Chris Coe; Walter Imber;
	Hong Kong Tourism Board
Cover Photo:	Jon Davison
Layout:	Media Content Marketing, Inc.
Cartography:	Raffaele De Gennaro

*Although the publisher tries to insure the accuracy of all the
information in this book, changes are inevitable and errors may
result. The publisher cannot be responsible for any resulting loss,
inconvenience, or injury. If you find an error in this guide, please
let the editors know by writing to Berlitz Publishing Company,
400 Alexander Park, Princeton, NJ 08540-6306.*

ISBN 2-8315-7833-7

Printed in Italy
010/201 REV

CONTENTS

• A ☛ in the text denotes a highly recommended sight

Hong Kong

HONG KONG AND ITS PEOPLE

Exciting, mysterious, glamorous—these words have described Hong Kong for at least a century. With its vibrant atmosphere and night-and-day activity it is an intoxicating place. Hong Kong is crowded—it has one of the world's greatest population densities. But it is also efficient, with one of the best transportation systems anywhere, and for such a crowded place, quiet—you don't hear voices raised in anger, motorists sitting on their horns, or loud boomboxes. Shopping never ends—there's always another inviting spot just down the street. You'll find Hong Kong easy to get around, the people helpful, English spoken everywhere, and food that lives up to its reputation.

On 1 July, 1997 the British Crown Colony of Hong Kong reverted to Chinese sovereignty as a Special Administrative Region of the People's Republic of China. Today Hong Kong remains a capitalist enclave with its laws and rights intact, and China has promised that Hong Kong will continue in this fashion for at least 50 years. Beijing's announced policy of maintaining Hong Kong's prosperity and stability makes sense. Hong Kong has long been China's handiest window on the West, and the city is unrivaled in its commercial know-how and managerial expertise. Around the time of the transition there was much speculation about how things would change. But in fact, once news of the handover vanished from the front pages, the people of Hong Kong returned to their usual topics of conversation: the economy and the price of housing.

The impression of the visitor today will be that very little has changed. Establishments are no longer called "Royal," Queen Elizabeth has vanished from the coinage, and the

Chinese traditional music continues to thrive in Hong Kong, especially among the older set.

Union Jack has been replaced by the flag of China and the new Hong Kong flag with its bauhinia flower. But in fact, there have been changes, many of them due to economic progress, new construction, and other factors that influence cities all over the world.

Others are more subtle. British social customs are still evident in the kind of polite service you get in hotels and in the long lines of people waiting for buses at rush hour. The British population has decreased; today there are as many American and Australian ex-pats as there are British.

With a population of nearly eight million and a total area of just over 1,095 square km (423 square miles), housing is one of Hong Kong's perennial nightmares. To alleviate the problem, the government has become the city's major landlord with the construction of massive apartment blocks that, though they have every modern facility, average only 9 square m (100 square ft) in size. Whole cities have been created in the New Territories, although the unimaginative architecture of these towns has been criticized.

Of Hong Kong's population, 98 percent are Chinese. The majority are Cantonese, born in Hong Kong, or from South China, but there are immigrants from all over China. The Chinese people have been described as hardworking and pragmatic, attitudes that have contributed to Hong Kong's success. There are many stories of refugees who arrived with nothing in their pockets, set up a small sidewalk stall, worked diligently until they had their own store, and then expanded it into a modest chain.

Old customs are still followed: Fate and luck are taken very seriously, and astrologers and fortune-tellers do a steady business. Before a skyscraper can be built, a feng shui (see page 68) investigation must take place to ensure that the site and the building will promote health, harmony, and prosperity. You'll also notice that gambling is a passion, whether it be cards, mah-jong, the lottery, or the horses. Hong Kong has two major racetracks as well as an intensive off-track betting system, and on weekends the ferries to Macau are crowded with people on their way to the casinos.

Sightseeing in Hong Kong starts at sea level with the enthralling water traffic—a mix of freighters, ferries, tugs, junks, and yachts. Views of the city and the harbor are panoramic. From Victoria Peak, Hong Kong's highest

Even after repossession by China, it's still business as usual in Hong Kong.

point, or from skyscrapers and hotels, they are especially exciting at night when the lights are on.

The business and financial center and the signature soaring architecture are on Hong Kong Island. Across Victoria Harbor, connected by ferry and the MTR rail line, is the Kowloon peninsula with its hotels, nightlife, and almost non-stop shopping. Beyond, in the New Territories, are a mixture of high-rise suburban towns, ancient sites and walled villages, country parks, and farms with ducks and fish ponds. Hong Kong's other, less developed islands, Lantau, Lamma, and Cheung Chau, provide getaways. You can also take a ferry to Macau to find an entirely different kind of city, a unique blend of Chinese and Iberian culture.

It's anyone's guess what may happen in the future, but for now Hong Kong bristles with energy and ambition, and for the visitor, this beautiful city with its contrasts and variety is an exhilarating experience.

Across the harbor, the tightly packed skyline of Kowloon's Kwun Tong district shimmers at dawn.

A BRIEF HISTORY

In the popular mind, the history of Hong Kong, long the entry-way to China for Westerners, begins in 1841 with the British occupation of the territory. However, it would be wrong to dismiss the long history of the region itself. Archaeologists today are working to uncover Hong Kong's past, which stretches back thousands of years. You can get a glimpse into that past at Lei Cheng Uk Museum's 1,600-year-old burial vault on the mainland just north of Kowloon (see page 38). In 1992, when construction of the airport on Chek Lap Kok was begun, a 2,000-year-old village, Pak Mong, was discovered, complete with artifacts that indicated a sophisticated rural society. An even older Stone Age site was discovered on Lamma Island in 1996.

While Hong Kong remained a relative backwater in early days, nearby Guangzhou (Canton) was developing into a great trading city with connections in India and the Middle East. By A.D. 900, the Hong Kong islands had become a lair for pirates preying on the shipping in the Pearl River Delta and causing a major headache for burgeoning Guangzhou; small bands of pirates were still operating into the early years of the 20th century.

In the meantime, the mainland area was being settled by incomers, the "Five Great Clans": Tang, Hau, Pang, Liu, and Man. First to arrive was the Tang clan, which established a number of walled villages in the New Territories that still exist today. You can visit Kat Hing Wai and Lo Wai, villages with their walls still intact. Adjacent to Lo Wai is the Tang Chung Ling Ancestral Hall, built in the 16th century, which is still the center of clan activities.

The first Europeans to arrive in the Pearl River Delta were the Portuguese, who settled in Macau in 1557 and for several centuries had a monopoly on trade between Asia, Europe, and South America. As Macau developed into the greatest port in the East, it also became a base for Jesuit missionaries; it was later a haven for persecuted Japanese Christians. While Christianity was not a great success in China, it made local headway, evidenced today by the numerous Catholic churches in Macau's historic center. Intermarriage with the local Chinese created a community of Macanese, whose culture can still be seen in Macau's architecture and cuisine.

The British Arrive

"Albert is so amused," wrote Queen Victoria, "at my having got the island of Hong Kong." Her foreign secretary, Lord Palmerston, was not so amused; he dismissed Hong Kong as "a barren island with hardly a house upon it."

Hong Kong Island formally became a British possession two years later in 1843. The British now had a base for the thriving trade they had carried on from Canton. Trading conditions, however, were not easy. The attitude expressed by Emperor Qianlong at Britian's first attempt to open trade with China in 1793 continued to prevail: "We possess all things," said the emperor, "I set no value on objects strange or ingenious, and have no use for your country's manufactures."

Moreover, China would accept nothing but silver bullion in exchange for its goods, so Britian had to look for a more abundant commodity to square its accounts. Around the end of the 18th century, the traders found a solution: Opium was the wonder drug that would solve the problem. Grown in India, it was delivered to Canton, and while China outlawed the trade in 1799, local Cantonese officials were always willing to look the other way for "squeeze money" (a term still used in Hong Kong).

In 1839 the emperor appointed the incorruptible Commissioner Lin Tse-hsu to stamp out the smuggling of "foreign mud." Lin's crackdown was indeed severe. He demanded that the British merchants in Canton surrender their opium stores, and to back up his ultimatum he laid siege to the traders, who, after six tense weeks, surrendered over 20,000 chests of opium. To Queen Victoria, Lin addressed a famous letter, pointing out the harm the "poisonous drug" did to China, and asking for an end to the opium trade; his arguments are unanswerable, but the lofty though heartfelt tone of the letter shows how unprepared the Chinese were to negotiate with the West in realistic terms.

A year later, in June 1840, came the British retaliation, beginning the first of the so-called Opium Wars. After a few skirmishes and much negotiation, a peace agreement was reached. Under the Convention of Chuenpi, Britain was given the island of Hong Kong, and on 26 January 1841, it was proclaimed a British colony.

The Opium Wars

The peace plan achieved at Chuenpi was short-lived. Both Peking and London repudiated the agreement, and fighting resumed. This time the British forces, less than 3,000 strong but in possession of superior weapons and tactics, outfought the Chinese. Shanghai fell and Nanking was threatened. In the Treaty of Nanking (1842) China was compelled to open five of its ports to foreign economic and political penetration, and even to compensate the opium smugglers for their losses. Hong Kong's status as a British colony and a free port was confirmed.

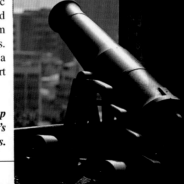

An old cannon conjures up the violent past at Macau's historic Monte Fortress.

In the aftermath of the Opium Wars, trade in "foreign mud" was resumed at a level even higher than before, although the major traders, by now respectable and diversified, stopped their trading in 1907. Opium-smoking continued openly in Hong Kong until 1946; in mainland China the Communist government abolished it when they came to power in 1949.

Commerce and Wealth

The first governor of Hong Kong, Sir Henry Pottinger, predicted it would become "a vast emporium of commerce and wealth." Under his direction, Hong Kong began its march toward prosperity. It was soon flourishing; with its natural harbor that attracted ships, Hong Kong leaped to the forefront as a base for trade. Both the population and the economy began to grow steadily. A surprise was the sizable number of Chinese who chose to move to the colony.

In the meantime, the opening of Hong Kong was the last blow to Macau's prosperity. Inroads had already been made by the arrival of the Dutch and Macau's loss to them of the profitable Japanese trade. From then on, until its 1970s comeback with electronic and other export goods, Macau sank into obscurity.

Despite the differences between the Chinese majority and the European minority, relations were generally cordial. Sir John Francis Davis, an early governor, disgusted with the squabbling of the English residents, declared: "It is a much easier task to govern the 20,000 Chinese inhabitants of the colony than the few hundreds of English."

There were a few incidents: On 15 January 1857, somebody added an extra ingredient to the dough at the colony's main bakery—arsenic. While the Chinese continued to enjoy their daily rice, the British, eating their daily bread, were dropping like flies. At the height of the panic, thousands of Chinese were deported from Hong Kong. No one ever discovered the identity or the motive of the culprits.

Conditions in the colony in the 19th century, however, did not favor the Chinese population. The British lived along the waterfront in Victoria (now Central) and on the cooler slopes of Victoria Peak. The Chinese were barred from these areas, and from any European neighborhood. They settled in what is now known as the Western District. It was not uncommon for several families and their animals to share one room in

Speaking Chinese

While Chinese can be called the world's most widely spoken language, it actually has innumerable dialects—people from Beijing can't understand a word people from Hong Kong say; in fact they can't even understand people from Shanghai. What has bound the country together over thousands of years is the written language.

Each Chinese character represents an idea—a meaning, not a sound. There are about 50,000 characters; some 5,000 of these are in common use. Writing a single character may require from 1 to 33 strokes. Written Chinese is a subtle language—choice of one character over another can convey delicate shades of meaning. Handwriting style is also important —the Chinese consider calligraphy a serious art form. Chinese is traditionally written in columns, read from top to bottom and right to left. However, today you often see printed Chinese characters presented much like a European language.

Putonghua, or Mandarin, is China's official language and is gradually becoming the lingua franca all over mainland China. Cantonese is spoken in Hong Kong and South China. While putonghua has only four tones, Cantonese uses up to seven different tonal inflections to distinguish otherwise identical syllables. This makes Cantonese an especially difficult language for foreigners to learn.

crowded shantytowns. So it is not surprising that when bubonic plague struck in 1894, it took nearly 30 years to fully eradicate it. Today in the Western District, you can still wander narrow streets lined with small traditional shops selling ginseng, medicinal herbs, incense, tea, and funeral objects.

In 1860, a treaty gave Britain a permanent beach-head on the Chinese mainland—the Kowloon peninsula, directly across Victoria harbor. In 1898, under the Convention of Peking, China leased the New Territories and 235 more islands to Britain for what then seemed an eternity—99 years.

The 20th Century

The colony's population has always fluctuated according to events beyond its borders. In 1911, when the Chinese revolution overthrew the Manchus, refugees flocked to the safety of Hong Kong. Many arrived with nothing but the shirts on their backs, but they brought their philosophy of working hard and seizing opportunity. Hundreds of thousands more arrived in the 1930s when Japan invaded China. By the eve of World War II, the population was more than one and a half million.

A few hours after Japan's attack on the American fleet at Pearl Harbor in December 1941, a dozen Japanese battalions began an assault on Hong Kong; Hong Kong's minimal air force was destroyed on the airfield at Kai Tak within five minutes. Abandoning the New Territories and Kowloon, the defenders retreated to Hong Kong island, hoping for relief which never came. They finally surrendered on Christmas Day in 1941. Survivors recall three and a half years of hunger and hardship under the occupation forces, who deported many Hong Kong Chinese to the mainland. A number of Hong Kong's monuments were damaged during this time: St. John's Cathedral was turned into a military club, the old governor's lodge on the Peak was burned down, and the commandant of the occupation forces rebuilt the colonial governor's mansion in Japanese style.

At the end of World War II, Hong Kong took stock of what remained—the population was down to half a million, and there was no industry, no fishing fleet, and few houses and public services.

Hong Kong Comes Back

China's civil war sent distressing echoes to Hong Kong. While the Chinese Communist armies drove towards the south, the flow of refugees into Hong Kong multiplied, and by the time the People's Republic of

In a city already packed with buildings, new construction is constantly underway.

China was proclaimed in 1949, the total population of Hong Kong had grown to more than two million people. The fall of Shanghai in 1950 brought another flood of refugees, among them many wealthy people and skilled artisans, including the Shanghai industrialists who became the founders of Hong Kong's now famous textile industry. In the late 1970s Hong Kong became the conduit for China's goods, investment, and tourism. It also found itself famous as a worldwide bargain shopping center.

Housing was now in desperately short supply. Housing had always been scarce for Hong Kong's Chinese. The problem became an outright disaster on Christmas Day in 1953. An uncontrollable fire devoured a whole city of squatters' shacks in Kowloon; 50,000 refugees were deprived of shelter. The calamity spurred the government to launch an emergency program of public-housing construction; spartan new blocks of apartments put cheap and fireproof roofs over hundreds of thousands of heads. But this new housing was grimly overcrowded, and even a frenzy of construction couldn't keep pace with the demand for living space. In 1962 the colonial authorities closed the border with China, but even this did not altogether stem the flow of refugees: The next arrivals were the Vietnamese boat people.

Typhoon

No natural danger poses more of a threat to Hong Kong than a typhoon (dai fung or "big wind" in Cantonese). Typhoons always cause damage, and disastrous typhoons have occurred over and over throughout Hong Kong's history. Despite modern techniques of surveillance and early warning, there are casualties and damage almost every year. Typhoons generally occur between July and September.

A series of signals from one to ten alerts residents in the event of a storm. Signal No. 1 goes up when a tropical storm that could escalate into a typhoon has moved within a 460-mile radius of Hong Kong. People generally pay little attention at this point. Signals No. 3 and 4 mean that the winds have escalated, accompanied, perhaps, by heavy rains. Tours and harbor cruises are suspended, and some businesses close.

No. 8 is the most serious: It means that the gale has reached Hong Kong. Banks, offices, museums, and most shops and restaurants close, and all transport is suspended. In case of a No. 8 warning, you should remain in your hotel and check the storm's progress on TV or radio.

Into the 21st Century

As 1997 drew nearer, it became clear that the Chinese government had no intention of renewing the 99-year lease on the New Territories. Negotiations began, and in 1984 Prime Minister Margaret Thatcher signed the Sino-British Joint Declaration, in which Britain confirmed the transfer of the New Territories and all of Hong Kong to China in 1997. For its part, China declared Hong Kong a "Special Administrative Region" and guaranteed its civil and social system for at least 50 years after 1997. Although China's Basic Law promised that Hong Kong's existing laws and civil liberties would be upheld, refugees began flowing the other way. The British Nationality Act (1981) had in effect prevented Hong Kong citizens from acquiring British citizenship, and thousands of people, anxious about their future under China's rule, were prompted to apply for citizenship elsewhere, notably in Canada and Australia. The protests in 1989 in Beijing's Tiananmen Square sparked sympathy marches in Hong Kong, and further increased tension with China. Some companies moved their headquarters out of Hong Kong.

Ironically, as the handover approached, the British granted the Hong Kong Chinese more political autonomy than they had done since the colony was founded, including such democratic reforms as elections to the Legislative Council.

Since the handover in July 1997, China has generally followed a hands-off policy. Many who fled have returned. What controls heartbeats in Hong Kong are the fluctuations of the Hang Seng Index, foreign currency exchange rates, and skyrocketing property prices. In short, the status quo prevails. Everybody hopes Hong Kong will remain stable, but everyone also has their doubts. In the meantime, the philosophy is to seize present-day opportunities in the thriving economy.

WHERE TO GO

The crowded Kowloon peninsula and the booming New Territories on the mainland call for some serious sightseeing; but we begin across Victoria Harbor on Hong Kong Island, where the city was first founded and which remains the center of government, business, and commerce.

HONG KONG CENTRAL

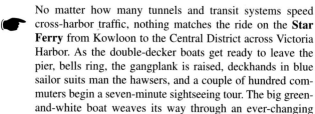

No matter how many tunnels and transit systems speed cross-harbor traffic, nothing matches the ride on the **Star Ferry** from Kowloon to the Central District across Victoria Harbor. As the double-decker boats get ready to leave the pier, bells ring, the gangplank is raised, deckhands in blue sailor suits man the hawsers, and a couple of hundred commuters begin a seven-minute sightseeing tour. The big green-and-white boat weaves its way through an ever-changing obstacle course of both large and small craft, and the soaring **skyline** of Hong Kong Island draws nearer.

As you get off, the 52-story **Jardine House** with porthole-shaped windows catches the eye. There are restaurants and a Starbuck's in the basement, and you can access the raised pedestrian crosswalk from the escalators on the ground floor. Next to the Jardine building is Exchange Square, a complex with a large shopping mall; just behind it is the General Post Office with a philatelic center on the ground floor.

Farther west is the ferry terminal for the outlying islands. On Connaught Road Central, you'll find one of Hong Kong's curiosities, the 244-m- (800-ft-) long **Mid-Levels outdoor escalator.** It ferries commuters from the Mid-Levels apartment complexes downhill from 6 to 10am, and uphill from 10am to midnight. Nearby is Central Market, the wholesale food market of Hong Kong, and the Hang Seng building (private offices).

Just east of the Star Ferry terminal, you'll come to **City Hall.** No longer a center of government, it now functions as a cultural center. Go through the underground walkway to **Statue Square;** on the east side of the square is the **Legislative Council Building,** one of the few colonial buildings left in Hong Kong. So great is the pressure on the available land that most of Hong Kong's colonial architectural heritage has been demolished and replaced by new skyscrapers. Despite protests by preservationists, there was little alternative.

Nearby is **Chater Garden** and a number of notable architectural landmarks. Most famous is the striking 74-story **I.M. Pei Bank of China Tower,** not beloved by the people of Hong Kong — its triangular prisms and sharp angles violate the principles of feng shui (see box, page 68) and its radio masts stick up like an insect's antennae. The rival

A ride across Victoria Harbor on the Star Ferry is an unforgettably exhilarating experience.

Modern architecture and bad feng shui meet in the I.M. Pei Bank of China Tower.

Hong Kong and Shanghai Bank is by architect Norman Foster; built on a "coathanger frame," its floors hang rather than ascend. From inside the vast atrium you can view the whole structure as well as the mechanical workings of the building. Two bronze lions, carrying out feng shui principles, guard its doors.

You can catch one of Hong Kong's historic **trams** along Des Voeux Road and ride from Central to Causeway Bay (see box, page 66). In 1904, the narrow, double-decker trams ran along the waterfront, but land reclamation has placed them far inland.

From the Bank of China Tower, make a short detour up Garden Road and turn into Battery Path to reach the landmark **St. John's Cathedral.** Built 1847–1849, this usually deserted Anglican foundation is Hong Kong's oldest church. During World War II, the church was turned into a club for Japanese officers; it was restored after the war. Note the stained glass windows in the Quiet Chapel, designed by Joseph Edward Nuttgens in the late 1950s. Behind the church is the 1917 French Mission Building, now used as the Court of Final Appeal.

Across from the I.M. Pei tower a winding path leads up to **Hong Kong Park.** The park's 10.5 hectares (25 acres) of landscaped gardens and lakes contains a large **greenhouse** that holds many species of plants, and an **aviary** of exotic birds. In the park is the **Flagstaff House Museum of Tea Ware** (see page 54). It's in Hong Kong's oldest colonial building, with exhibits describing the history of tea from the Warring States period (475–221 B.C.) to the present.

If you leave the park and walk up Cotton Tree Drive, you will find the Peak Tram terminal.

TO THE SUMMIT

For more than a century, the most exhilarating way up **Victoria Peak** has been by funicular. The **Peak Tram** starts its scenic climb just across the street and around the corner

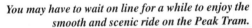

You may have to wait on line for a while to enjoy the smooth and scenic ride on the Peak Tram.

from the American Consulate in Garden Road and makes its way, sometimes at a startlingly steep incline, to the summit at 398 m (1,305 ft). The right-of-way travels past fancy apartment blocks, bamboo stands, and jungle flowers. Passengers crane their necks for dizzying glimpses of the harbor. The Peak is still the most fashionable place to live in Hong Kong, but real estate prices here are astronomical; rents run around HK$50,000 a month.

The Peak Tram, originally steam-powered, was built to speed the wealthy *taipans* to their mountainside retreats. Before the tram was built, sedan chairs and rickshaws were the only way to get here. Since the tram's inauguration in 1888 it has stopped only for typhoons and World War II.

The modern 120-passenger cars make the journey in around eight minutes. However, on sunny Saturdays and Sundays you may have to brave a crowd lining up at the

The views of the city from Victoria Peak are especially breathtaking at night.

lower terminal. During the spring and autumn festivals, when people traditionally seek out the hilltops, the throngs are so large you would be better advised to try another time.

At the upper terminus there is a four-level shopping center, the Peak Galleria, and the Peak Tower, which resembles an airport control tower and has shops, entertainment, and restaurants.

You can **walk around the peak** for impressive views of Hong Kong, the coastline, and the islands in 45 minutes on Lugard and Harlech roads. The view is especially effective at night. There are also souvenir stands, benches for a rest, and perhaps Hong Kong's last surviving rickshaws — however these are not for rides, but are a tourist photo opportunity. If you're up to a climb, take the Mount Austin road to the **Victoria Peak Gardens.** These gardens used to belong to the governor's mountain lodge, but the building was demolished by the Japanese during the occupation of Hong Kong.

From the lower terminal of the Peak Tram it's only a short walk to the former governor's residence, Government House, now a museum. Across from the mansion, the **Zoological and Botanical Gardens** (gardens open daily 6am–10pm; zoo 6am–7pm; admission free) provide a welcome oasis amid the big-city pressures. In the very early morning the park is taken over by people doing tai-chi exercises. Both young and old go through ballet-like movements in slow motion to discipline the mind and body. The park's zoo has a collection of weird and wonderful chattering jungle birds.

MORE HONG KONG ISLAND SIGHTS

Western District

The Western District is one of Hong Kong's oldest neighborhoods, and its narrow streets hold a collection of fascinating traditional shops and enterprises. Opposite the Macau Ferry

The Peak Galleria and Peak Tower offer restaurants, shopping, entertainment, and spectacular views.

Terminal you'll find the **Western Market** (open 10am–7pm). It is more interesting for its architecture than for its shopping; it's situated in a four-story Edwardian building built in 1906. For an interesting glimpse of small and family-owned shops, walk along Bonham Strand East and West, Man Wa Lane, and Cleverly Street. You'll find herb and medicine shops, incense shops, chop makers' shops (makers of Chinese seals), and more.

Hong Kong University's campus is spread along Bonham Road. When it opened in 1912, the university had a total of 72 students. At the top of a sloping driveway, the stately Edwardian structure that was the original university building presides over the institution's newer buildings. The University's **Fung Ping Shan Museum,** 94 Bonham Road (open

Monday–Saturday 9:30am–6pm, admission free) holds a significant collection of antiquities: bronzes, dating from 3000 B.C., and ceramics, including Han Dynasty tomb pottery. It also has the world's largest collection of Nestorian crosses from the Yuan Dynasty period.

Around Hollywood Road

Take the Mid-Levels Escalator to Hollywood road, known for its antiques and curio shopping. Here the windows and open doors of the shops reveal an alluring selection of Asian furniture, carpets, carvings, tomb figures, porcelain, and bronze.

Walk west along Hollywood Road until you come to **Man Mo Temple,** the island's oldest house of worship (though the date of its founding is subject to dispute). Visitors entering the temple are confronted by a dense pall of smoke from all the burning joss sticks and the incense coils hanging from the ceiling (these will burn for as long as a month). The gold-plated sedan chairs on the left-hand side of the temple were once used for trans-

> The Chinese put their family name first, followed by the given name.

porting the statues of the temple's gods in religious processions. The statues in the main shrine represent Man, the god of literature, and Mo, the god of war, a curious juxtaposition. The temple is always crowded with worshipers.

Just past the temple is the aptly named Ladder Street. Go down one flight of steps to Lascar Row, popularly known as **Cat Street,** for more antiques and curio shops. Walk up the steps to reach Caine Lane, where you'll find the **Museum of Medical Sciences** (open Tuesday–Saturday 10am–5pm; admission by donation). The interesting Edwardian building was formerly the Pathological Institute, founded to combat the 19th century's 30-year-long outbreak of bubonic plague. The

Maiden's Rock, site of the annual Maiden's Festival, appears to mimic the trajectory of distant skyscrapers.

old laboratory is still intact, and there are exhibits on Chinese pharmacology and the history of medicine in Hong Kong.

Wan Chai

Just to the east of the financial district, Wan Chai was once an area of sleazy clubs and topless bars; this was the setting for *The World of Suzy Wong*. Servicemen relaxing from the rigors of the Vietnam War poured millions of dollars into the Wan Chai boom of the 1960s. There are still bars and clubs here, but the area has become almost mainstream, and office towers are replacing many of the sinful old premises.

The Wan Chai waterfront is dominated by the **Hong Kong Convention and Exhibition Centre,** the largest in Asia, which includes hotels, theaters, and exhibition halls. The convention center, an extension on reclaimed land, affords stunning views of the Wan Chai waterfront. Adjacent, just west of the convention center, is another modern highlight, the **Academy for the Performing Arts** on Gloucester Road.

On Wan Chai's Bowen Road, Maiden's Rock, also called Lover's Rock, is the gathering place for the annual Maiden's festival. Although it is not a tourist attraction, the rock is steeped in tradition. Every August young women convene to light joss sticks and some even climb the nine-meter (30-ft) rock to pray for good husbands.

Causeway Bay

About 2 km (a mile) east of Wan Chai, Causeway Bay is second only to Tsim Sha Tsui as Hong Kong's place to shop. A prosperous tourist district, it is full of shopping centers and department stores, along with a number of good restaurants. The busy night-and-day crowds make this area vibrant and lively.

On the nautical side is the Causeway Bay **typhoon shelter,** where expensive yachts are anchored almost gunwale to gunwale, and the Hong Kong Yacht Club has its headquarters. Across Gloucester Road, opposite the World Trade Centre, is the **Noonday Gun,** which under British rule was sounded on the stroke of midday. Silent for a time, the tradition has been revived and is a tourist attraction. It's not clear how the custom started. One story has it that traders Jardine, Matheson & Co fired a private salute for a visiting tycoon, an act that incensed the colonial authorities, who felt that they had the sole right to issue such a 21-gun welcome. As a result, the merchants were forced to limit their salvoes to one a day — and from then on, they signaled the noon hour daily for all to hear. The gun was made famous by Noel Coward's satirical song, "Mad Dogs and Englishmen."

Farther east is Hong Kong's largest park, **Victoria Park,** with sports grounds and other facilities. On the eastern side of Victoria Park on Causeway Road is **Tin Hau Temple,** dedicated to Tin Hau, the Taoist Queen of Heaven and patroness of seafarers. Originally the temple was on the shore but reclamation projects have now left it high and dry. On the 23rd day of the Third Moon, the birthday of the goddess is celebrated here and in all Hong Kong fishing communities.

Inland from the bay is **Happy Valley.** At one time it was a very miserable valley, a swampland conducive only to breeding malarial mosquitoes. It is home to Hong Kong's first racetrack. Hong Kong's gamblers are so eager to play the horses that, despite the opening of a bigger and better racetrack at Sha Tin, the **Happy Valley Racecourse** is thriving.

> It's important to have a visiting card in China — present your card with both hands.

Up Tai Hang Road behind Causeway Bay is Aw Boon Haw (Tiger Balm) Gardens (open daily 9:30am–4pm), founded in 1935 by the late Aw Boon Haw, who became a millionaire by producing the medicinal Tiger Balm. (It does not, in fact, contain any ingredients from tigers, but does promise to cure a wide range of problems such as colds, headaches, rheumatism, gout, toothache, and scorpion bites.) With its garish pagodas, artificial caves, and brightly painted statues of well-known Taoist and Buddhist legends, the garden is an obvious photo opportunity.

AROUND THE COAST

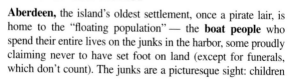

Aberdeen, the island's oldest settlement, once a pirate lair, is home to the "floating population" — the **boat people** who spend their entire lives on the junks in the harbor, some proudly claiming never to have set foot on land (except for funerals, which don't count). The junks are a picturesque sight: children frolicking on the poop deck, women preparing food or playing mah-jong, elderly folk watching the sunset, dogs and cats underfoot, songbirds in bamboo cages overhead — and all afloat.

The boats may appear deceptively primitive, but many of them have their own electric generators and all the modern conveniences. There are fewer boats now than in the past; many boat people, especially the younger generation, have moved to housing projects. You can take a tour of the port in one of the small **sampans,** propelled by hand by women drivers. A half-hour tour costs HK$50; pay at the end, or the driver may cut your trip short.

Aberdeen's theatrical **floating restaurants** have been a tourist attraction for many years. The food may not live up to

Once infamously seedy, Wan Chai got a needed touch of class with the Hong Kong Convention and Exhibition Centre.

expectations, but the fantasy environment makes up for it. If you can get up early enough, you can attend the pre-dawn auction held at the vast local wholesale **fish market;** otherwise, have a look at the street market that goes on later in the day.

The peninsula opposite the east coast of Ap Lei Chau island contains **Ocean Park** (open daily 10am–6pm; admission HK$150 adults, HK$75 children), which has become one of Hong Kong's biggest attractions. It is divided into three areas: a highland, a lowland, and the Middle Kingdom. Linking the lowland and highland sections of the park, a cable-car system offers spectacular views across to the islands of the South China Sea.

The Oceanarium is said to be the largest in the world, and the Ocean Theatre features displays by dolphins, killer whales, seals, and pelicans. An enormous roller-coaster rising way above the sea, space wheels, and high-diving shows guarantee a day of excitement. The Middle Kingdom is a recreated "living" history of China's past, presented through a number of full-size replicas of shrines, temples, pagodas, palaces, and street scenes. There are also demonstrations of traditional Chinese crafts, including silk-weaving, pottery, and papermaking. Water World, formerly in the complex, has closed for redevelopment.

Continuing around the coast in a counter-clockwise direction, Deep Water Bay offers a good beach and harbors. The next inlet is **Repulse Bay,** a roomy, sandy crescent, with green hills. It's so attractive and so easy to reach that it's packed with sunbathers all summer long.

Stanley was once one of the main fishing villages on Hong Kong Island. The well-known **Stanley Market** (see page 55) is a major source for bargain clothing and other merchandise. Stanley is also a favorite place of residence for ex-pats. The waterfronts at Repulse Bay and Stanley are lined with good cafés and restaurants.

A cruise ship passes before Causeway Bay, a district alive with plenty of dining and shopping opportunities.

KOWLOON

Though much smaller than Hong Kong Island, Kowloon has almost twice the population. In many areas, the density reaches the equivalent of 150,000 inhabitants per square km (a quarter square mile).

Most of Kowloon's attractions for visitors are centered near the tip of the peninsula in the district known as **Tsim Sha Tsui.** Adjacent to the Star Ferry terminal is **Ocean Terminal,** where international cruise ships dock, and the gigantic **Harbour City,** a complex of malls, hotels, and restaurants.

If you walk east on the Star Ferry terminal concourse, you will find yourself on the wonderful **Promenade,** which begins at the clock tower, all that remains of the once grand Kowloon-Canton Railway Terminus. The waterfront here

Repulse Bay is an easy destination for sun worshippers seeking a respite from the big city.

offers unparalled views of the harbor and Hong Kong Island. If you continue to the end of the promenade, you will be in Tsim Sha Tsui East, a busy commercial district built on more than 60 hectares (150 acres) of reclaimed land.

Flanked by the clock tower is the imposing **Hong Kong Cultural Centre.** Hong Kong's major venue for the performing arts, the building has been criticized for its fortress-like architecture and windowless façade. The interior is a comfortable amalgam of Chinese and Western design, with an impressive main lobby. The center contains a concert hall with acclaimed acoustics, theaters, a library, an exhibition gallery, shops, restaurants, and bars.

Next door is the **Hong Kong Space Museum and Theatre** (open Monday, Wednesday–Friday 1–9pm; Saturday, Sunday

10am–9pm; closed Tuesday; admission HK$10 adults, HK$5 children; separate admission to theater). Its futuristic dome design is striking; inside are interactive exhibits, including one in which you can experience weightlessness. The theater presents "sky shows" and IMAX films. The **Hong Kong Museum of Art** (see page 54) stands behind the Space Museum next to the cultural center. It contains the Xubaizhi collection of painting and calligraphy; galleries devoted to antiquities and ceramics; and a gallery of modern Chinese art. Particularly interesting is the collection of paintings and photographs of old Hong Kong. The museum mounts special exhibitions and has an excellent gift shop.

A few blocks up Chatham Road South are two more major museums. The **Science Museum** (see page 55) is a state-of-the-art interactive museum that will teach you how everything and anything works from ancient sailing ships to the latest technology. The **Museum of History** (open Tuesday–Saturday 10am–6pm, Sunday 1–6pm; closed Monday; admission HK$10 adult, HK$5 child) opened its new permanent collection at the end of August 2001. The fascinating collection of artifacts

Stanley's waterfront is full of peaceful settings offering food and drink with a view.

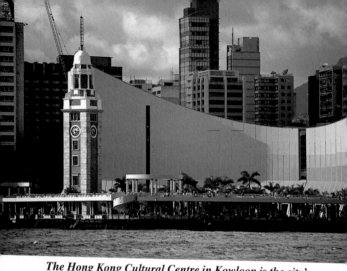

The Hong Kong Cultural Centre in Kowloon is the city's unofficial headquarters for the performing arts .

showcases 6,000 years of Hong Kong's history and Chinese culture.

Just across Salisbury Road from the cultural center is the historic **Peninsula Hotel,** now expanded and modernized by a 32-story tower. Its restored lobby is Hong Kong's most elegant gathering place; afternoon tea here is a visitors' ritual.

Alongside the hotel runs busy **Nathan Road,** Hong Kong's fabled shopping street, lined with shops, hotels, and restaurants. Kowloon's main street was created by Sir Matthew Nathan when he was governor of Hong Kong at the turn of the 19th century. At the time it was built, many thought it absurd to have a tree-lined boulevard running through what was practically a wilderness. Now the former "Nathan's Folly" is known as the "Golden Mile."

A few blocks up Nathan Road is **Kowloon Park** (open daily 6am–midnight), elegantly laid out with fountains, promenades, and ornamental gardens; be sure to go up the steps to see the Sculpture Walk.

Farther up Nathan Street you will reach **Yau Ma Tei**, one of the older parts of Kowloon. Turn off Nathan and walk down Kansu Street to find the **Jade Market** (open 10am–3pm; see page 80), with more than 100 stalls spread out in a large tent, just before you reach the overpass.

Hong Kong's liveliest market scene is the **Temple Street Night Market** (see page 55), near Jordan Road. Everything is sold here, from clothing to souvenirs to electronic goods, and the market is known for its street-side food stalls, where you can dine inexpensively on seafood. The market runs all the way up to **Tin Hau Temple,** where you will find fortune tellers' tables (some speak English) and possibly street performers singing Chinese opera or pop songs. The temple is one of the many dedicated to Tin Hau, goddess of sea-farers; this one also houses an altar to Shing Wong, the city's god. In the daytime the temple (open 8am–6pm) attracts worshipers, and its park attracts strollers and mah-jong players.

Explore the great unknown at the Hong Kong Space Museum and Theatre.

Nathan Road goes all the way up to **Boundary Street,** which marks the boundary between Kowloon and the New Territories. Near Boundary Street, off Prince Edward Street West, is the **Yuen Po Street Bird Garden** (open 8am–7pm). Birds are favorite pets in Hong Kong, valued for their singing rather than their plumage, and here you'll find all kinds of birds for sale as well as elaborate teak and bamboo cages.

Off the beaten path in Sham Shui Po, west of the junction of Nathan Road and Boundary Street, is the **Lei Cheng Uk Han Tomb and Museum** on Tonkin Road (open Monday–Wednesday and Friday–Saturday 10am–6pm, Sunday 1–6pm; closed Thursday). This ancient burial vault is believed to date back to the Han Dynasty (A.D. 25–220). The barrel-vaulted chambers were discovered while excavating for a nearby housing project.

NEW TERRITORIES

Hong Kong's New Territories begin at Boundary Street. Surprises spring up on all sides: new industrial complexes alongside sleepy farming villages, skyscraper towns blooming in the middle of nowhere, Hakka women in their traditional flat straw hats with hanging black curtains, water buffalo, and flashes of azalea everywhere.

The Hong Kong Museum of Art features ancient as well as modern collections.

The Science Museum offers lots of interactive exhibits and educational presentations.

The New Territories can be explored by taking the **Kowloon–Canton Railway** (KCR), which makes 10 stops between the station in Kowloon and Sheung Shui, the last stop before entering China. Ask the tourist authority about its interesting **Heritage Tour** from Kowloon and other countryside tours (see page 113).

The main highway makes a circuit of the New Territories, beginning with the new town of Tsuen Wan, situated in an area of heavy industry just west of Kowloon. North of the town, a commanding view over all the New Territories to the north can be seen from **Tai Mo Shan,** Hong Kong's highest peak at 957 m (3,140 ft). The highway continues parallel to the coast. One-third of all Hong Kong's beaches are to be found in a single 14-km (9-mile) stretch of this region's shoreline. Place names are often based on the distance to the nearest mile-post,

On Nathan Road, Kowloon traffic may reach a standstill but it never lets up.

as measured from the tip of the Kowloon peninsula. Thus you will find "19½-mile Beach" at Castle Peak Bay.

The main road continues clockwise around the New Territories. As you approach the border, you can glimpse the skyscrapers of Shenzhen. The lookout point at Lok Ma Chau was once known as Hong Kong's "window on China" — in the years of China's isolation from the West, tourists would come to the lookout point here and rent binoculars in order to get a glimpse of the great mystery beyond.

Set amid Tseun Wan's residential towers is the 18th-century walled village of **Sam Tung Uk,** now preserved as a museum, and a short walk from the MTR station. Not far away, at milepost 21 near the large new town of Tuen Mun, is a Taoist retreat known as **Ching Chung Koon.** This "Temple of Green Pines" is a spacious complex containing temples and pavilions, statues, and gardens. It is known for its collection of bonsai and houses a jade seal more than 1,000 years old. Among the ponds is one inhabited by turtles: Visitors toss in coins in the hope of bouncing one off a turtle's head, a sure way of achieving good fortune.

An even more interesting image out of Chinese history is the walled village of **Kat Hing Wai,** in the village of Kam Tin just outside the market town of Yuen Long. This is the most easily accessible of the New Territories' walled villages. It is built in a square, and the only way in is through the gate in the brick defensive wall. Kat Hing Wai was built four or five centuries ago by the Hakka Tang clan, one of the Five Great Clans that migrated here from North China (see page 11). Many of the old houses in the village have been replaced by modern structures.

The Tang clan's earliest walled village was **Lo Wai**, which also has its defensive wall intact and is entered by a narrow gate. Adjacent to the village is the restored **Tang Chung Ling**

Neon signs light up the night as throngs of people crowd the sidewalks along Kowloon's Nathan Road.

Ancestral Hall. Few traditional ancestral halls remain in China since the anti-historical destruction during the Cultural Revolution, so these New Territories ancestral halls are rare survivors. Another such hall, belonging to the Liu Clan, is Liu Man Shek Tong in the village of Sheung Shui.

☞ One of the most interesting sites in the New Territories is **Tai Fu Tai,** another rare survivor, this one a mansion that belonged to a Confucian high official. The house was built in 1865 by a member of the Man clan who achieved the rank of *tai fu* (mandarin) by doing well in the Imperial Examinations. The preservation of this wonderful home is ongoing; a projected restoration of the original garden is still in progress. The traditional Qing Dynasty style of the mansion is enlivened by a few Western touches: a Baroque-style ceiling and stained glass above the doorways, showing the builder's up-to-date attitude at the time of construction.

The highway and the railway stay close together from Fanling, site of the best golf courses in the area. Tai Po, just south of Fanling, is known for its market, **Tai Po Market,** which buzzes with activity daily from 7am to 6pm. Just up a lane from the market is the **Man Mo Temple,** with long-burning incense coils hanging from its ceiling, a popular spot dedicated to the Taoist gods of war and literature.

The railway line then curves gracefully around Tolo Harbor, an idyllic body of water well-protected from the open sea. You can take a ferryboat through the harbor, past the ingenious Plover

> Hong Kong people are among the world's highest per capita users of cellular phones — one in five persons owns one.

Cove reservoir, a water catchment area appropriated by damming and draining a broad inlet from the sea. The boats go on to the friendly fishermen's island of Tap Mun, in Mirs Bay, with stops in remote hamlets of the **Sai Kung Peninsula.**

The Sai Kung area is the location of two official parks and nature preserves, while on the south side of the peninsula are some of the territory's best beaches.

From the next railway station, the modern campus of the Chinese University of Hong Kong is visible. Teaching here is conducted in both Chinese and English. The Art Gallery in the Institute of Chinese Studies Building is worth a visit for its painting and calligraphy collections.

Sha Tin is the site of the **Monastery of 10,000 Buddhas,** which looks down on a burgeoning town. There are hundreds of stone steps in the hillside to walk up before you reach **Man Fat Temple** with its regiments of small gilt statues of Buddha

Visitors climb the nine-story pagoda at Man Fat Temple to enjoy the spectacular view.

lining the walls. Some indefatigable climbers will want to go up to the top of the nine-story pink pagoda for a panoramic view. There is a total of 12,800 Buddha statues here, plus the remains of the monastery's founder embalmed in gold leaf. Also here is the **Hongkong Heritage Museum** (call Tel. 2180 8188 for open hours). The museum has an art collection, and displays of toys and other artifacts.

The giant Tiantan Buddha looks majestically over the Po Lin monastery of Lantau Island.

Down to earth, the **Sha Tin Racecourse** can accommodate over 80,000 spectators and is equipped with every imaginable luxury, including a giant video screen facing the stands, and for the horses, air-conditioned stables. Opposite the Sha Tin railway station, **New Town Plaza** features shops, cinemas, and even a computer-controlled musical fountain.

Two natural rock formations are always pointed out on excursions. Sha Tin Rock, better known as **Amah Rock,** is actually a pile of several rocks that resemble a woman with a baby in a sling on her back. Legend has it that a local woman climbed the hill every day to watch for her husband returning from across the sea; one day the wife and her child were turned to stone as a permanent symbol of her enduring faith. Closer to town is **Lion Rock,** shaped like a lion lying in wait. It really looks the part; the tourists know its name even before the guide can translate it.

THE ISLANDS

Excursion companies sell a variety of orientation cruises of Hong Kong harbor that include a look at some of its 235 outlying islands. These pleasant, but expensive, outings can lay the foundation for your own explorations aboard the cheap but usually comfortable ferries used by the islanders themselves. From the ferry terminals on Hong Kong Island you can escape to islands without cars or cares, where the local people smile "hello" and, if you're lucky, point you to a secret beach for the ultimate in quality leisure time. For ferry information, call Tel. 2542 3081 or 2525 1108.

Lantau Island

The mountainous island of Lantau is the biggest in the colony, and covers nearly twice the area of Hong Kong Island. Chek Lap Kok airport sits on reclaimed land just off Lantau; plans to build a bridge may change Lantau, but at present it is sparsely populated and makes a perfect getaway.

At 934 m (3,064 ft), Lantau Peak is high enough to attract the occasional rain cloud — refreshingly cool breezes blow on most hot summer days. More than half the island is parkland, and there is a 70-km (45-mile) circular **hiking trail** (see page 92). Ferries depart from Central every two hours between 6:10am and 10:30pm to Silvermine Bay (Mui Wo), where a bus terminal has buses to all parts of the island. There are also ferries to Discovery Bay.

A short bus ride away is **Cheung Sha Beach,** 3 km (2 miles) long, and popular for its white sand and excellent facilities.

The most famous site on the island is the world's tallest seated bronze statue of Buddha at 22 m (72.6 ft), the

Tiantan Buddha (see page 55). The statue and a small museum are on a peak, up 268 steps, above **Po Lin Monastery.** The monastery is strictly vegetarian, and visitors are warned not to bring any meat with them. You can have a delicious vegetarian lunch here.

From the monastery, hikers enjoy the two-hour cross-country trek down to Silvermine Bay, but the authorities have warned walkers to be on the lookout for snakes, which can be plentiful in the Lantau hinterland, especially in summer. The hillsides that surround the monastery are the site of Hong Kong's only tea plantation. Visitors are welcome to visit the 24-hectare (60-acre) establishment, and may sample the end product, Lantau tea.

Some 25,000 people are packed onto the tiny island of Cheung Chau, most of them living simple lives.

The island's largest community is **Tai O.** The people of this picturesque village make their living by fishing, duck-breeding, and food-processing. Many of the inhabitants live — by choice, not necessarily through economic hardship — on the water, aboard houseboats or in houses on stilts in the main creek.

A **Trappist monastery,** situated on a hillside overlooking the east coast of Lantau, is also open to visitors. To get here, follow the path from the southwest end of Discovery Bay; the walk takes about 30 minutes.

Cheung Chau

Some 10 km (6 miles) west of Hong Kong lies this small, crowded island, only one square mile in size. More than 25,000 people live here, mostly by fishing, but there are also ex-pats, attracted by its laid-back Mediterranean ambience.

Pak Tai temple, dating back to 1783, is one of the primary attractions of Cheung Chau.

The island has a checkered past of smuggling and piracy. That era is gone now, but other elements of the island's old life are preserved. The people still carve jade and build sea-

Strolling down Pak She Pray Road is a fitting way to adjust to the easy, slow-going life on Cheung Chau.

worthy junks, all by hand. Fish (heads discreetly wrapped in paper) are still hung out to dry in the sun.

Cheung Chau becomes the center of Hong Kong life once a year, usually in May, during the **Bun Festival,** a folklore extravaganza (see page 89). The rest of the year, life goes on at its accustomed pace: rickety machines chugging in two-man factories, children in school uniforms being ferried home to houseboats, and the old fishermen stirring shrimp paste.

By way of formal tourist attractions, **Pak Tai Temple,** built in 1783, has some fine carvings and a great iron sword said to be 600 years old. But the most interesting thing to do here is to explore the two villages on the island, **Cheung Chau** and **San Wai.** They are an easy walk apart by the harbor road, or a longer 45-minute hike on the scenic Peak Road. The **Praya,** the promenade in front of the ferry pier, is a good place to observe the many junks and fishing boats in the harbor. There are also several open-air restaurants where you can enjoy fresh seafood.

Fishing is the primary source of income on laid-back Cheung Chau Island.

Lamma Island

Only 35 minutes by ferry from Central, Lamma Island is perfect for swimming, hiking, picnicking, birdwatching, or just sitting back to watch the bananas grow. Hong Kong's third largest island has a population of only about 12,000; it is still largely undeveloped, and life on Lamma, if not totally primitive, is close to the essentials. Archaeologists indicate that Lamma has probably been inhabited for some 4,000 years, and the island is known as "Hong Kong's Stone Age Island."

The principal settlements are **Yung Shue Wan** on Lamma's northwest, and **Sok Kwu Wan,** on the east coast.

Both villages offer good waterfront restaurants with home-style Chinese food, principally seafood fresh from the tank. The ports are within hiking distance of several beautiful beaches, and within a one-hour hike of each other on a marked trail. You can build an appetite for dinner by making your way from the beach to the restaurant. Yung Shue Wan is still a very British residential enclave, with many nice pubs.

AN EXCURSION TO MACAU

Macau, the final bastion of Portugal's great 16th-century empire, is much more than just a quirk of history. Here, where East and West first met, life combines the spirit of Asia with something of the sunny atmosphere of the Mediterranean.

A 35-minute ferry ride from Central, the trip to Lamma Island makes a fine excursion for hiking and hanging out.

Macau's **historic center,** with its colonial architecture, has a distinctly Mediterranean flavor. Colonnaded public buildings, iron balconies, winding streets, flagstoned squares and the many churches all speak of the Portuguese inheritance as well as the Chinese, a fusion of East and West that has produced the unique Macanese culture.

The story of the Western discovery of Macau begins in 1513 when Portuguese explorer, Jorge Alvares, reached the south coast of China. Traders followed in his wake, setting up bases in several parts of the Pearl River estuary. Finally, in 1557, they were all consolidated in Macau. It was the only European gateway to China, and through Macau flowed Western technology

> In giving gifts, avoid objects considered unlucky, like clocks, anything colored white, blue, or black (including wrapping), or sharp implements.

and religion. In 1576 Pope Gregory XIII created the Macau diocese, covering all of China and Japan.

No less impressive were the secular challenges. China and Japan were not on speaking terms, so trade between them had to be channeled through a neutral middleman. Lucky Macau fit the specifications exactly. Portugal's resulting near-monopoly of East–West trade understandably awakened the competitive instincts of other European powers. The Dutch sent an invasion flotilla to Macau in 1622, but the defenders triumphed. However, the end of the golden age was drawing near. China began to relax trade restrictions, and with the rise of Hong Kong, Macau became an isolated Portuguese outpost.

A haven for persecuted Japanese Christians in the 17th century, Portugal's neutrality during World War II assured the territory a flood of refugees. They were joined by a swarm of spies of all conceivable nationalities, and Macau

Behind the façade of this Macau hotel, casino tables are busy 24 hours a day.

won a name for international intrigue.

Portugal's very precarious foothold on the Asian coast ended in 1999 with a formal handover to China. Macau, now the Chinese Special Economic Zone of Zhuhai, is becoming something like a boomtown as an exporter of toys, furniture, and electronics. New construction in the past 10 years has changed the city's skyline; with new, glittering hotels and highrise apartment blocks, the city is beginning to look a little more like Hong Kong.

Macau's population is estimated at around 450,000, an appallingly high figure for such a small area; recent land reclamation has eased the situation to some extent. If a trace of tropical lethargy still adds to the charm in this city of sidewalk cafés, palm trees, and pedicabs, any torpor definitely ends once inside the doors of Macau's casinos, scene of some of the liveliest gambling west of Las Vegas. Gambling provides almost 40 percent of the government's tax revenues, and is a major source of employment. Its spin-off industries, prostitution and pawn shops, also thrive.

Arriving

The easiest way to get to Macau is by jetfoil, operated by TurboJet (Tel. 2859-3333). The 40-mile trip takes about an hour. Departures are from the Macau Ferry Terminal, just west of Central in the Shun Tak Centre, 200 Connaught Road, Central, in Hong Kong. Jetfoils leave every 15 to 30 minutes 24 hours a day.

Entry procedures are similar to those in Hong Kong — most nationalities need only a passport to enter Macau. Macau's own currency, the pataca, is pegged to the Hong Kong dollar, and you can use your Hong Kong currency freely in Macau.

Upon arrival in Macau, be sure to stop by the Macau Government Tourist Office for a map, brochures, and directions. Outside the terminal, you will find taxis as well as buses to all points (take 3, 3A, 10, or 10A to the historic center; exact change is required). You'll also be approached by pedicab drivers; these are tricycles carrying two passengers. Pedicabs were once the most common form of transportation in Macau, but today they are mainly a tourist attraction.

Wild and Beautiful

Remote areas of the New Territories and sections of Lantau Island are happy sighting grounds for birdwatchers. Hundreds of species have been recorded, from everyday egrets and funny-faced cockatoos to mynahs and pelicans. The Sai Kung Peninsula Nature Preserve has many hiking trails for the nature lover.

As civilization encroaches, wild animals have been vanishing: leopards have not been seen in 20 years. But you can still come across barking deer, monkeys, porcupines, and scaly anteaters. In the wilderness you may also stumble upon a banded krait, a cobra, or some other fearsome snake. Though sightings are common, bitings are rare.

Hong Kong Highlights

Aberdeen. *Hong Kong Island, South. Bus: 7 or 70 from Central bus terminal.* The harbor is crowded with the junks of the boat people. At night, fantastic floating restaurants, strung with lights, offer a unique atmosphere. (See page 30)

Flagstaff House Museum of Tea Ware. *Victoria Barracks, Cotton Tree Drive, Central; Tel. 2869 0690.* In Hong Kong's oldest colonial building, an unusual collection of Chinese tea sets dating from the fifth century B.C. to the present. Thurs–Tues, 10am–5pm, closed Wed; admission free. (See page 23)

Historic Trams and Ferries. The Star Ferry has been taking people from Kowloon to Hong Kong Island's Central District since 1898. A ride on one of Hong Kong's double-decker trams is a sightseeing tour of Hong Kong Island's streets. (See pages 20 and 22)

Hollywood Road. *Central. Take Mid-Levels Escalator.* Hong Kong's most famous antiques street, with shops selling beautiful porcelain, rosewood furniture, carpets, and chinoiserie. (See page 27)

Hong Kong Museum of Art. *Cultural Centre, Tsim Sha Tsui; Tel. 2734 2167. MTR: Tsim Sha Tsui.* A fine collection of traditional Chinese art and ceramics, along with modern art galleries, as well as special exhibitions. Fri–Wed, 10am–6pm; admission HK$10 adults, HK$5 children and seniors. (See page 35)

Kat Hing Wai Walled Village. *Kam Tin, New Territories. Bus: 51; Ferry: Tsuen Wan ferry from Sheung Wan.* A glimpse of ancient China: The narrow streets of this 17th-century settlement with its defensive wall, are still occupied by descendants of its builders. (See page 41)

Macau's historic center. *Macau. Ferry: From the Macau ferry terminal; for information, Tel. 2859-3333.* The narrow, winding streets present a unique blend of Portuguese and Chinese architectural and cultural influence. (See page 51)

Po Lin Monastery. *Lantau Island. Ferry from Central, then Bus 2 from Mui Wo.* Buddhist monastery with a colorful setting below the world's largest seated bronze statue of Buddha. Daily 10am–6pm; vegetarian lunch, noon–4pm, HK$60–HK$100. (See page 46)

Promenade. *Tsim Sha Tsui.* A walk along the waterfront, with marvelous views of the harbor with its crowded boat traffic and the lofty Hong Kong Island skyline. (See page 33)

Science Museum. *2 Science Museum Road, off Chatham Road South, Tsim Sha Tsui; Tel. 2732 3232. MTR: Tsim Sha Tsui.* An interactive state-of-the-art museum with more than 500 exhibits, most of them hands-on. Tues–Fri 1–9pm; Sat, Sun 10am–9pm, closed Mon; $HK25 adult, $12.50 child). (See page 35)

Stanley Market. *Stanley, Hong Kong Island South. Bus: 6 or 260 from Central bus terminal.* Lively outdoor markets and bargain buys in a picturesque fishing village. 10am–6pm. (See page 32)

Temple Street Night Market. *Temple Street, Kowloon. MTR: Jordan.* Hong Kong's most famous market, with a lively bargaining scene, fortune tellers, street entertainers, and food carts. 7am–10pm. (See page 37)

Victoria Peak and the Peak Tram. *Central, Tel. 2522 0922 for tram.* A thrilling ride takes you up Hong Kong Island's highest mountain, home of the rich and famous. Superb views over Hong Kong and the islands any time, but especially at night. (See page 23)

Sights in Macau

Directly across the street from the wharf where passengers arrive from Hong Kong is the first surprise to greet visitors to Macau — the vast Jai-alai Palace, said to be the world's most luxurious *frontón*. In an effort to provide yet one more thing to bet on, players are imported from Spain to take part in this lightning-fast Basque ball game.

The grandstand situated on the seaside road, the Avenida da Amizade (Friendship Avenue), marks the finishing line for the Macau Grand Prix, the international car-racing event held here every November. Also in front of the ferry terminal

Running through the hills of Hong Kong's outlying areas is a good way to release the stress of the city.

is a new Cyber fountain, with 86 water spouts that shoot up to 70 m (230 ft) and are illuminated at night by 288 spotlights producing 80 colors.

Continuing around the peninsula in a clockwise direction brings you to the Rua da Praia Grande (Big Beach Street) — a pleasant promenade with shaded benches under the banyan trees. Along this elegant avenue is Government House, a modest pink palace.

The central square of the historic city center is **Largo do Senado.** For an authentic feel of old Portugal, slip into the cool entrance hall of the impressive **Leal Senado** ("Loyal Senate" building), a

> Although there are numerous Chinese dialects, the written characters are the same everywhere.

fine example of colonial architecture. On the inside walls are flowered blue tiles (*azulejos*) and coats of arms. The inscription over the archway reads, *"Cidade do nome de Deus, não ha outra mais leal"* ("City of the Name of God, None is More Loyal") — a bit of praise attributed to Portugal's King John IV in the 17th century. For all its historic grandeur, the loyal Senate now is the equivalent of a city council, its statesmanship dedicated to water supplies, sewage lines, and the establishment of playgrounds.

Macau's most memorable monument is the Baroque façade of the ruins of **São Paulo,** the only remains of a beautiful 17th-century Jesuit church. On top of a hill in the center of the city, it's approached by a grand staircase. The rest of the building and an adjoining college were destroyed in a typhoon-fanned fire in 1835. The rich sculptural effects on the façade mix Eastern and Western symbols: familiar saints, Chinese dragons, and a Portuguese caravel. Beneath the church, the Museum of Sacred Art houses a collection of sacramental objects.

The ambitious **Museum of Macau** (open Tuesday–Sunday 10am–6pm; admission HK$15) opened in 1998 in the lower levels of the Monte Fortress. Entrance is by escalator, near St. Paul's. It gives an overview of Macau's history and its daily life and traditions. A re-created street of colonial Macau is lined with traditional Chinese shops. The fort, built by the Jesuits in the 17th century as a defense against the Dutch, was largely destroyed by the same fire that burned St. Paul's.

Luís Vaz de Camões (1524–1580), the Portuguese national poet whose work immortalized that country's golden age

of discoveries, may have stayed in Macau. Local legend claims that he wrote part of his great saga, *Os Lusíadas*, in what is now called the **Camões Grotto,** situated in the spacious tropical Camões Garden.

Next to the museum, behind a gate (opened to anyone who knocks), is the Old Protestant Cemetery. Those whose fate was to die on some far foreign field could not have wanted a more peaceful, lovely graveyard. The small, whitewashed chapel was the first Protestant church built in China.

It's all a façade — you're certain to remember a trip to the ruins of São Paulo.

For a different vision of Old China, spend a few quiet moments in the classic **Lou Lim Ieoc Garden.** Here, arched bridges, pagodas, fish ponds, and stands of bamboo create the mood of a timeless Chinese painting. Nearby is the **Memorial House of Dr. Sun Yat-sen,** founder of the Chinese Republic. Photos and documents tell the life story

Hong Kong Glossary

Getting around is difficult when place names are pronounced differently in English and Cantonese. Kowloon (which means Nine Dragons) is pronounced more or less the same in both languages, but other names can be a problem. To give you a head start, here are 15 troublemakers: in the first column, the customary English name, in the second column, the approximate Cantonese pronunciation. And if that fails, point to the Chinese characters in the third column.

Aberdeen	**Heung Gong Jai**
Causeway Bay	**Tung Lo Wan**
Central District	**Jung Wan**
Cross Harbor Tunnel	**Hoi Dai Sui Do**
Happy Valley	**Pau Ma Dei**
Ocean Park	**Hoi Yeung Gung Yuen**
The Peak	**San Deng**
Peak Tram	**Lam Che**
Post office	**Yau jing guk**
Railway station	**Fo che jam**
Repulse Bay	**Chin Sui Wan**
Stanley	**Chek Chue**
Star Ferry Pier	**Tin Sing Ma Tau**

of the physician-revolutionary-statesman, who lived for a time in Macau, but never in this building.

Kun Iam Tong, off Avenida do Coronel Mesquita (open daily 8am–6pm), is a 17th-century Buddhist temple of considerable splendor and charm. Surrounded by statues, carvings, and incense burners, here the faithful make their devotions and check their fortunes, and traditional funerary displays give a cheerful send-off to the recently departed.

An unexpected piece of historical memorabilia turns up in the monastery garden, where guides point out a small stone table used for a treaty-signing ceremony in 1844. The signatories, who were the Chinese viceroy from Canton and the minister plenipotentiary of the United States of America, put their names to a historic document — the first-ever treaty between the two countries.

Another important ceremony took place in 1999 when Macau became part of China. The **Handover Pavilion** was meant to be a temporary structure, but public outcry ensured its preservation (located on Xian Xing Hai; open weekdays 10am–6pm, until 10pm weekends). Nearby is the Macau Cultural Center and the **Museum of Art** (open Tuesday–Sunday 10am–7pm; closed Monday; small admission).

Macau's oldest museum, the **Maritime Museum** (Wednesday–Monday 10am–5:30pm; admission HK$10, HK$5 children over 10) traces the history of Macau's connection to the sea. Exhibits cover fishing, seaborne trade, sea transport, and there is an aquarium. The museum also offers boat tours aboard a fishing junk.

The museum is almost on the spot where the Portuguese first landed. When they came ashore they found the **A-Ma**

A fruit market offers a bounty of exotic produce that locals take for granted.

Temple (properly called Ma Kok Temple; open daily dawn to dusk), dedicated to the favorite goddess of fishermen, who is also known as Tin Hau. The area was called *A-Ma Gau* ("Bay of A-Ma"), and in this way, Macau got its name. The ornate, picturesque temple dates from the Ming Dynasty (1368–1644) and is the oldest building in Macau.

The remains of the 17th-century Barra Fortress, which once defended the southern tip of the peninsula, contains the chapel of Santiago (St. James). The saint is much revered in

> When making a request of a Chinese person, it is best to be indirect, allowing the recipient to refuse without embarrassment.

the surrounding area. Among other legends surrounding the statue is a very modern one: During the Chinese Cultural Revolution, when Red Guards were running rampant on Wanchai island, just a swim away, the image of St. James is said to have stepped down from the altar and halted an invasion. Part of the fortress has been converted and is now used as a luxury inn. The northernmost point in Macau is the frontier between two contrasting worlds. The Barrier Gate (*Portas do Cerco*), which was built more than a century ago, marks the boundary between the enclave of Macau and the People's Republic of China.

Trying Your Luck

Macau's casinos are a source of non-stop excitement. There are 12 of them; you can't miss the eye-popping Lisboa, which has several floors of gambling, but there's also the Hyatt Regency, the Mandarian Oriental, and Taipa's Jockey Club. The fancifully decorated Macau Palace, a floating casino moored on the western waterfront, is fitted out with gambling tables, slot machines (known locally as "hungry tigers") and, for hungry humans, a restaurant. Gambling is

Bicycling is a preferred mode of transportation in China, but impractical in the traffic of Hong Kong and Macau.

wildly popular with the Chinese of Hong Kong, and they make up nearly 80 percent of all visitors to the casinos.

The casinos offer familiar international games — baccarat, blackjack, boule, craps, roulette — along with more exotic Chinese pastimes. Watch the fantan dealer for a few minutes and you'll almost be an expert: It's simply a matter of how many odd buttons are left after he has divided a pile of them into groups of four.

Dai-Siu (Big and Small) is a dice game in which the croupier throws three dice inside a glass container. Players bet on the numbers that will come up, and on whether the result will be "big" or "small." *Keno* is a variation of bingo in which the player chooses numbers to bet on before the draw is made.

The casinos have no admission charge and formal dress is optional, though long pants for men are required. They keep busy 24 hours a day, but if you want a change of scene there are always more gambling opportunities available. You can try your luck at pari mutuel betting on jai-alai at pari mutuel, greyhound-racing at the Canidrome (one of the largest in the world), and harness-racing on Taipa.

Shopping in Macau

Like Hong Kong, Macau is a duty-free port. It is famous for its gold jewelry. Market prices per tael (34 grams/1.2 ounces) of gold are set daily. You should always ask for a certificate of guarantee when you buy gold or jewelry. Look for jewelry shops along Avenida do Infante D. Henrique and Avenida de Almeida Ribeiro.

Browsing is a real pleasure in Macau's main streets and byways, where shops aimed at the tourist market are interspersed with the more workaday ironmongers, herbalists, and noodle stalls. Knowledgeable visitors look for antiques — either Chinese heirlooms or leftovers from the gracious Portuguese colonial days. However, you are not likely to find bargains, and you should be aware that unless you are an expert, you can end up with a fake. Also worth investigating are contemporary handicrafts, both Portuguese and Chinese, from across the border.

Food and Drink

Gourmets award Macau high marks for dependable Chinese cooking with an exotic bonus: Portuguese food and wines. Macau's own cuisine is a combination of Chinese flavors with the flavors imported from Portugal, Brazil, and Africa. Whether you choose to dine in one of the Macanese, Chinese, traditional Portuguese, or international-style restaurants, you will be treated to a hearty meal at a good price.

The ingredients, especially the fresh fish and seafood, are first-rate. A delicate, delicious fish is Macau sole (*linguado*). Imported dried cod (*bacalhao*) is the Portuguese national dish; several varieties are available, usually baked.

Macau has an ample supply of Portuguese wines. Try a *vinho verde*, a mildly sparkling young wine from northern Portugal, or a hearty red *Dão* or *Colares*. After dinner, a glass of Madeira or port is recommended to round off the meal. The more abstemious can stick to Portuguese mineral water.

Taipa and Coloane

Bridges link Macau with its two islands. Since the construction of the New Macau-Taipa Bridge has allowed easy

The Macau-Taipa Bridge makes for easy passage between gambling-happy Macau and the mellower Taipa Village.

access to the airport, the population has grown to more than 30,000, with industrial development, new apartment blocks, and luxury resort hotels.

The quaint **Taipa Village,** with its narrow lanes and colonial buildings painted yellow, blue, and green, has almost been completely swallowed up by the development of nearby housing projects. The island is also the designated home of the University of East Asia. Pay a visit to the **Casa Museu da Taipa,** and you'll be able to get a glimpse of how Macanese families lived in former days. A grand colonial house, fully restored and outfitted with period furnishings, provides the centerpiece for this expanding "cultural village."

Take a Tram

The ancient trolley-car system that travels along Des Voeux, Hennessy, and Causeway roads is the most leisurely and revealing way to see Hong Kong. With more than 32 km (20 miles) of track, the jerky electric double-deckers cover almost the entire north coast of the island. Enter at the back of the tram, and try to get a seat in the front of the upper deck for the best views of Hong Kong's colorful streets, always crowded with shoppers and nonstop day-and-night activity. You'll pass through Wan Chai, where the world of Suzy Wong once existed, and travel all the way to the eastern extremity of Shau Kei Wan, once a pirates' hangout, and still with a colony of "boat people" who live on junks and sampans parked in the bay.

The western terminus is in Kennedy Town, an over-crowded section of the city, named after a 19th-century Hong Kong governor, Sir Arthur Kennedy. When you're ready to get off the tram, just drop your fare in the box at the front beside the driver. (see page 22)

The streets of Macau are rife with colonial history and architectual diversity.

Farther away is **Coloane,** connected to Taipa by a causeway and a large land reclamation project. Not as developed as Taipa, it offers the joys of sand and sea and is known for its beaches. Cheoc Van and Hac Sa ("Black Sands") are both popular resort areas, with lifeguards on duty in summer and windsurfing boards for rent. There are restaurants, swimming pools, and changing facilities. The village of Coloane is picturesque, with a central square lined with cafés. The waterfront drive parallels the shore of a Chinese island, and boats headed to China pass through the narrow waterway. The small Chapel of St. Francis Xavier is dedicated to the 16th-century patron saint of missionaries, and has on display the elbow of the saint, along with the bones of numerous Japanese and Vietnamese martyrs.

Seac Pai Van Park, on the west coast of the island is an interesting natural preserve with a Natural History Museum.

Feng Shui: Seeking Prosperity

Feng shui (sometimes fung shui in Cantonese) literally means "wind and water." An ancient system of divination, its purpose is to achieve harmony with the forces of nature and produce an environment conducive to health and prosperity. Arranging physical premises according to the principles of feng shui deflects evil forces and assures the welfare of the inhabitants. Anyone moving into a new apartment will call in a feng shui geomancer to determine the optimum position of walls, doors, and even furniture.

Buildings should face quiet water if possible, or have water nearby, such as a fish tank or a fountain. Lions and dragons are protective. The Hongkong and Shanghai Bank's doors are guarded by a pair of bronze lions, and the China Resources Building by its Nine Dragons Wall. The famous I.M. Pei tower, on the other hand, ignored feng shui principles, and is considered an untamed "dragon's den."

The dragons of Hong Kong must also receive consideration. New buildings must not block their accustomed pathways to the water, and in one case a new apartment house was constructed with a huge opening that would allow the dragons passage.

The Hong Kong Chinese are firmly and verbally committed to feng shui, and its principles are becoming popular in America. Inside China, however, visitors will find that such traditions are played down, perhaps in deference to what is considered a more "modern" attitude.

AN EXCURSION TO GUANGZHOU (CANTON)

Guangzhou was China's major seaport for 2,000 years and the center for European traders in the 19th century. The city still maintains its important gateway role. Ever since 1957 the Canton Trade Fair (officially the Chinese Export Commodities Fair) has attracted throngs of international business people every spring and autumn.

Guangzhou, with a population of more than 5 million, straddles the Pearl River — China's fifth longest — which links the city to the South China Sea. This waterway accounts for much of the local charm and excitement, as the daily drama of the ferryboats, junks, sampans, freighters — and even small tankers and big gunboats — unfolds right in the center of town. The river also irrigates the carefully tended surrounding farmlands, creating a beautifully lush, subtropical scene.

Depending on its pronunciation the word *ma* can mean "mother," "hemp," "horse," or "to curse."

Guangdong Province has some of China's most fertile land, and grows two crops of rice a year, along with vegetables of all kinds.

Guangzhou today is mostly about business and industry, featuring new development, skyscrapers, a whole new business area, and raised expressways. The scary traffic is a real experience — vehicles of all kinds jockey for position on crowded streets, missing each other by inches, and speeding on the freeways is rampant. Guangzhou is interestingly one of China's most prosperous cities, determinedly on the move into the modern world. It seems that the picturesque older sections with their old houses, narrow streets, and winding alleyways may not be around much longer.

Arriving in Guangzhou

There are many package tours to Guangzhou from Hong Kong (see page 113), and this may be the easiest way to visit the city. However, it's also easy to get to Guangzhou by train or ferry. Four comfortable express trains depart the Kowloon-Canton Railway (KCR) Station in Hung Hom, Kowloon, making the trip in less than two hours. Turbo Cat ferries leave the China Hong Kong City (CHKC) terminal twice a day; the journey takes two hours. Citibus also travels to Guangzhou from CHKC; there are five round-trips a day, taking 3 1/2 hours.

You will need a visa to enter China (see page 109 for information). Hong Kong currency is widely accepted in Guangzhou, or you can change your currency into RMB (yuan) at any bank or hotel. Note, however, that the exchange does not go the other way (see page 116).

Guangzhou, like Hong Kong, is primarily Cantonese-speaking, but many people also speak Mandarin. English is spoken in hotels and tourist destinations.

If you travel by train, you will arrive at the Guangzhou East Station, a large modern complex, which connects with the subway, buses, hotel transfer services, and taxis. The train station is in the newer business district; nearby is Asia's third-tallest building, at 83 stories, which will often be pointed out to you.

Sights in Guangzhou

Yuexiu Park, situated near the Trade Fair in the northern part of the city, is Guangzhou's largest; it covers a hilly 100 hectares (247 acres). The park is landscaped with lakes and gardens. In the park is the 1380 **Zhenhai Tower,** one of the city's oldest buildings. Actually a five-story

Zhenhai Tower, one of Guangzhou's oldest buildings, now houses the municipal museum.

pavilion on a hilltop, it contains a fine collection of historical exhibits. **Dr. Sun Yat-sen's Memorial Hall** honors the founder of the Chinese Revolution, flanked by his heroic statue in copper. Dr. Sun Yat-sen (1866–1925) began his political career in Canton. This enormous, modern version of a traditional Chinese building, with sweeping blue tile roofs, contains an auditorium big enough to seat 4,700 people. It was built in 1931 with contributions from overseas Chinese. The center of the park is the **Five Rams Statue.** It celebrates the founding of Guangzhou, when five spirits rode their goats down from the celestial realm to present the inhabitants of the city with their very first grains of rice.

Guangzhou's most important Buddhist monument is the 1,400-year-old **Temple of the Six Banyan Trees** (open 8am–5pm). Although the banyan trees that once flourished here are now no more, the often-restored complex has remained a focus of local Buddhist activities. Golden Buddha statues in several of Buddha's aspects adorn the temples, and overlooking them is the 17-story Flower Pagoda, a slender relic of the Song dynasty (A.D. 960–1279).

In the early Middle Ages, Canton had a significant Muslim population as a result of its trade with the Middle East. This explains the presence in Guangzhou of the **Huaisheng Mosque,** reputed to be China's oldest, and traditionally dated A.D. 627. Rebuilt in modern times, the mosque serves the small local community of Muslims. The modern minaret is known as the "Plain (or Naked) Pagoda," in contrast to the Flower Pagoda of the Buddhist temple.

Make a Wish

If you need to change your luck, visit the Wishing Tree in the lush valley of Lam Tsuen, near Tai Po in the New Territories. There are actually two wishing trees; the desiccated one, struck by lightning, is purported to be the real wishing tree, but the one near the road, a large banyan, is prettier. In any case, from the nearby temple you can secure an orange tied to swatches of red paper. Write your wishes on the paper, and see how high you can throw your orange into the tree. The higher it goes, the more chance you have of your wish coming true. There's also a wishing tree in the Zu Miao temple if you visit Foshan.

Chen Jia Ci, the Chen Family Institute (open daily 8:30am–5pm), was built in the late 19th century to promote arts and crafts. An architectural wonder, it is itself a beautiful piece of craftsmanship with its sculpture and carved stone balustrades. Porcelain friezes adorn the rooftops and ridgepoles, telling the story of the *Romance of the Three Kingdoms*. Inside is a collection of ceramics, carvings, and furniture. There is also a market and a porcelain shop.

A former Confucian temple is presently the home of the historic **National Peasant Movement Institute,** where the Chinese Communist Party trained its leaders in the 1920s. Mao Zedong himself

Water travel is prevalent around Hong Kong and greater China as well.

directed the institute in 1926, and gave lectures on geography, rural education, and "The Problem of the Chinese Peasantry." Zhou Enlai also taught here.

The atmosphere of 19th-century Canton is best evoked on **Shamian Island,** a haunting, nostalgic place in the Pearl River. This small formerly residential island, beautifully shaded by banyan trees, was the home of the closed community of the foreign colony in the era of "concessions." The bridges were barred by night with iron gates to keep the

Fortune-telling is one of many ancient Chinese traditions that continues in Hong Kong and its neighboring cities.

Chinese out. Its stately European-style buildings have since been restored, largely for use as government offices and foreign legations. The island also has Guangzhou's first modern luxury resort hotel.

A popular optional excursion is an hour's detour to Guangzhou Zoo, founded in 1958. It houses more than 200 animal species, most famous of which is the giant panda, and has an imaginative monkey mountain behind a moat.

Not to be missed is a visit to Guangzhou's famous open-air market, **Qing Ping.** Guangzhou is famous for its food. The Cantonese love to eat and have the reputation of eating almost anything that walks on four legs. The market bears this out: Along with the usual ducks and chickens, you will see for sale snakes, dogs, bats, and sometimes monkeys — all are highly prized as delicacies. More pleasantly, you can browse among lanes of antiques, flowers, herbs, fruit, gold-fish, songbirds, and more.

A Side Trip to Foshan

A very popular day-trip from Guangzhou goes to Foshan, a city of nearly 300,000 people, renowned for its handicrafts for more than a thousand years. The individual arti-sans' shops are no longer here, but you can visit a silk-weaving factory, a ceramics plant, and the Foshan Folk Art Studio, where you can observe workers making

> Chinese has no words for *yes* and *no*. The sentence, or the verb, is repeated in the affirmative or negative. In Hong Kong people some-times say "hai" meaning *yes*, and "m'hai," meaning *no*.

Chinese lanterns, carving sculptures, painting scrolls, and cutting intricate designs in paper. The Foshan Art Porcelain Factory has traditional designs, but also some attractive mod-ern pieces.

Foshan's most outstanding artistic monument is **Zu Miao,** the Taoist Ancestral Temple, a Sung dynasty establishment rebuilt in the 14th century and well worth visiting. Constructed in wood, brick, stone, ceramic, and bronze, this is a work of extravagant beauty, uniting many ancient art forms. The complex contains the oldest wooden stage in China, used by the Wan Fu Tai Chinese opera.

AN EXCURSION TO SHENZHEN

Shenzhen was China's first Special Economic Zone. Literally created out of rural farmland, it was set up in the 1970s as the answer to Hong Kong. From a population of 20,000 it has grown into a metropolis of 2.5 million, with tightly clustered skyscrapers and some of China's highest grossing industries.

Because Shenzhen is much cheaper than Hong Kong, it is a popular weekend destination for Hong Kong's Chinese, who come to relax, dine in its resorts, and play golf — Shenzhen hosted the World Cup of Golf in 1995. It is even becoming something of a commuter town — owning or renting an apartment here costs a fraction of what it would in Hong Kong.

Shenzhen is easy to reach — the KCR commuter train runs throughout the day, the trip taking about 40 minutes. Visitors need a visa to enter China, and must disembark at the border (now called "boundary") checkpoint, Lo Wai. City buses also go to Shenzhen. A Turbo Cat ferry makes a one-hour trip (7am–7pm) from Hong Kong's Macau Ferry Terminal to Shekou on the Natau Peninsula, which is part of the economic zone.

Shenzhen is a premier shopping center, and much cheaper than Hong Kong. It is known for its inexpensive (but well-made) knock-off designer goods. You can use your Hong Kong dollars here, so there's no need to change currency. Some places take credit cards, but cash is better for bargaining. Just across the border is the huge **Lo Wu City shopping mall,** to which you can walk; other shopping malls are nearby.

Shenzhen's main tourist attractions are its enormous theme parks. One of them — **Splendid China** — purports to show "all of China in one day." It contains elaborate replicas of China's chief monuments in impressive detail, including a scaled-down version of the Great Wall. The 24 **China Folk Culture Villages** represent China's ethnic variety; they feature craftspeople in traditional costumes along with folksong and dance performances.

In Shekou is a large Free Market, and an exhibition of Xian's terra-cotta warriors.

WHAT TO DO

SHOPPING

Inflation has taken its toll in Hong Kong. While it's no longer the bargain shopping destination it once was, there are still some good buys to be had. Since Hong Kong is a duty-free port and charges no sales tax, goods are cheaper here than in the country where they were made. On photographic equipment, electronic goods, and watches, you avoid the luxury tax payable in your home country. Specialty goods and souvenirs, often handmade, come from Hong Kong and elsewhere in China. Custom-made garments by skillful Hong Kong tailors are still much in demand and cost less than elsewhere for comparable garments. Note that alcohol and tobacco are both exceptions to Hong Kong's duty-free regime and are subject to tax.

You'll find that prices are about the same in Hong Kong Central and Kowloon, and somewhat cheaper in Causeway Bay, which caters to local shopping. Large shops on the fashionable thoroughfares tend to be more expensive than smaller "family" shops tucked away in the side streets.

Stores do not open until 10am or later, but shopping goes on into the evening, up to 9:30pm. Most shops are open seven days a week. Shops in Central are an exception; they generally close at 6pm and are not open on Sunday. The only holiday on which all commerce comes to a halt is the Chinese New Year in January or February.

Buyer Beware. Be aware that name brands, including electronics, are sometimes fakes, glass may be sold as jade, and that antique you bought may have been made last night. Always ask for a receipt that records information about the item, and if you buy an antique, be sure to get a certificate of authentication. Needless to say, avoid peddlers who approach you on the street and offer to take you to wondrous bargains.

The large department stores have fixed prices, but elsewhere you should ask whether there is a discount, especially if you buy several items in one shop. Compare prices before you buy any significant item. Always ask to see the manufacturer's guarantee when purchasing watches, cameras, and audio-visual and electronic equipment.

Note that when haggling, the merchant assumes you are prepared to pay cash. If, after concluding a deal, you try to pay with a credit card, he may then boost the price in order to cover the card charges.

It is advisable to shop at outlets that are members of the Hong Kong Tourist Association (HKTA), identified by a red junk logo. Membership imposes an obligation to maintain standards of both quality and service, and provides dissatisfied customers with an officially recognized channel for redressing complaints; the number to call is Tel. 2508 1234. Pick up a copy of HKTA's "The Official Dining, Entertainment & Shopping Directory" in which all member stores are listed.

Shipping. Many stores will pack and ship purchases. Ask if automatic free insurance is provided. If the goods are very valuable or fragile, it is a good idea to buy an all-risk insurance for the shipment. Packages sent to the

Shopping in Hong Kong can sometimes feel like a competitive sport.

US or to Europe generally take six to eight weeks by surface mail, and one week by airmail.

Shopping Areas. Major shopping areas are Tsim Sha Tsui in Kowloon, especially along Nathan Road; Central on Hong Kong Island, particularly for upscale designer goods; Causeway Bay for slightly better prices; and the Hollywood Road area.

Department Stores. Look for Lane Crawford Ltd., an upscale store with branches at Pacific Place, 70 Queen's Road, and Harbour City; Wing On, one of the oldest in Hong Kong; Marks and Spencer; and the Japanese department stores, Mitsukoshi, Sobo, and Seibu.

Malls. Hong Kong is full of giant malls. Harbour City, just west of the Star Ferry Terminal in Tsim Sha Tsui is one of the largest; Pacific Place, 88 Queensway, is Central's biggest mall, with retail outlets and department stores; Times Square is a collection of retail outlets in Causeway Bay. In addition, most topline hotels have upscale malls full of designer boutiques.

Factory Outlets. These stores sell excess stock or factory overruns. Hong Kong is no longer a factory outlet center since much of its clothing manufacturing has moved elsewhere. There are factory showrooms in the Pedder Building, 12 Pedder Street, in Central.

Markets. Markets are the places to use your bargaining skills. Hong Kong's most

> In mid-July, Fashion Week brings parades and events to shopping centers around the city.

famous and colorful market is the **Temple Street Night Market** near the Jordan MTR stop. Every conceivable kind of goods is sold here: clothing, all kinds of electronics, CDs, souvenirs, crafts, and jewelry.

Stanley Market is located on Hong Kong's southern coast, and is well-known for all kinds of clothing, including silk and cashmere. Bargain, and carefully examine any merchandise you buy here.

79

The **Jade Market,** on Kansu Street in Yau Ma Tei, is known for both jade and freshwater pearls. This is not the place to make expensive purchases, but it's great for inexpensive pendants, earrings, and gifts.

What to Buy

Antiques. Hollywood Road in the Mid-Levels above Central is the most famous antiques street in Hong Kong. Look for fine Chinese bronzes, embroidery, lacquerware and porcelain, tomb figures, and wood carvings, among other possibilities. The experts point out that it is not age alone that determines a Chinese antique's value—the dynasties of the past had their creative ups and downs. For serious antiques, try Honeychurch Antiques at no. 29 for furniture and silver, Tai Sing Company at 122 for porcelain. For fun you can visit the Low Price Shop at no. 47 or the Cat Street crafts stores and flea market.

Brocades and Silks. Fabrics from China are a bargain and well worth taking home. Chinese-product department stores stock silk fabrics, silk scarves, finely embroidered blouses, and traditional padded jackets. Chinese Arts and Crafts is at Pacific Place in Central, and in Star House in Tsim Sha Tsui; CRC Department Store is on Hennessy Road in Causeway Bay. For fabrics, also try Western Market, Morrison Street, in Central.

Cameras. Photo buffs know that Hong Kong is the place to buy some of the world's most advanced photographic equipment, and there are some real bargains around. However, be sure you compare prices and models before buying. Two reliable places to start looking in Lan Kwai Fong are Photo Scientific in the Eurasia Building and Hing Lee Camera Company, 25 Lyndhurst Terrace.

Carpets and Rugs. Hong Kong is a mecca for Chinese hand-knotted wool carpets and silk rugs. Hong Kong's stores are usually able to arrange shipment. Caravan at 65 Hollywood Road and the shops in The Silk Road at Ocean Center in Tsim Sha Tsui are good places to start looking.

China (Porcelain). In Hong Kong you can have a plate, or even a whole dinner service, hand-painted to your own design. Factories in Kowloon and the New Territories, producing traditional and modern china, are geared to entertain and instruct visiting tourists; prices are appealing. Two of the largest places to go are the Wah Tung China Company in the Grand Marine Industrial Building in Aberdeen; and the Overjoy Porcelain Factory in Block B of the Kwai Hing Industrial Building, Kwai Chung, in the New Territories. In antiques shops, look for highly valued porcelains from China. Note that because of the duty-free situation, good bargains may be found in European china, including Spode and Wedgwood.

Electronics. The latest gadgets are sometimes available in Hong Kong before anywhere else. Before you begin shopping, pick up HKTA's "Shopping Guide to Consumer Electronics."

Tailor-made clothes are not as popular as they once were, but Hong Kong still offers fine custom dresses and suits.

Prices on electronics have risen in the past two years; check prices at home before you buy here. Nathan Road has many electronics shops. Also check out Star Computer City in the Star House near the Star Ferry terminal.

Furniture. The choice ranges from traditional hand-carved Chinese rosewood furniture to well-made reproductions of modern Western styles. Rattan furniture is highly popular. Hollywood Road has several furniture shops. Queen's Road East in Wan Chai is a furniture manufacturing and retail area.

Jade. "Good for the health" is just one of the many magical qualities that are attributed to these beautiful emerald-green or turquoise stones. Real jade is extremely expensive, and you may be offered counterfeit jade, which looks exactly like the genuine article. Some people say you can test the authenticity by touch—real jade feels smooth and cool. Alternatively, you can shine a lamp on the stone—real jade shows no reflected light. Better still, go shopping with an expert.

Jewelry. Thanks to the duty-free situation, prices in Hong Kong are lower than they are in some other places. You can buy gemstones loose or set, or have them made up to your own design. Popular purchases include diamonds and freshwater pearls. If you do plan to buy jewelry, be sure to consult the "Shopping Guide to Jewellery" published by the Hong Kong Tourist Authority to find a reputable dealer.

Kitchen Equipment. Woks and any other gadgets essential for Chinese cookery make good purchases. Department stores sell all sorts of intriguing kitchen equipment.

Leather Goods. Leather is not a great bargain in Hong Kong. Locally made items do not live up to their European models. However, the leather garment industry is growing, and there is a wide range of locally produced leather accessories, all at extremely attractive prices. For European imports, you will pay top dollar.

Musical, Audio, and Video Equipment. Hong Kong has a vast range of the most high-tech audio-visual, sound, and screen equipment. Before purchasing, visitors should make sure of compatibility with systems in their own countries. Be sure to look around and compare before buying. Whatever you buy, you may be able to work out a discount.

Ready-to-wear Clothes. Hong Kong's shops carry almost every recognizable European and many American labels, from top-end designers to the moderately priced or trendy. Nathan Road, Central, and the hotel malls are places to look. There are still a great many factory outlet stores with reasonable prices. You'll also find bargain clothes for sale at the markets and on push-carts.

Tailoring. Tailor-made clothes are not as popular in Hong Kong as they were in the past, but hundreds of shops still remain. Local tailors are experts when it comes to producing custom-tailored garments for both men and women, and are also adept at copying patterns. The result can be a quality suit at a fair price—but made-to-measure clothing is not cheap. In choosing a tailor, look for HKTA membership. Many tailors have Web sites or are listed on Web sites.

Tea. Shops all over town will sell you gift tins of exotic blends. If you want to learn

Jewelry is always a coveted commodity for commerce-driven Hong Kong visitors.

something about tea, go to the Tea Shop at 149 Hollywood Road, or the Moon Garden Tea House at 5 Hoi Ping Road, Causeway Bay. The owners will brew up a pot so you can taste before making a choice.

Watches. The saying "Time is money" is quite literally true in Hong Kong: more is spent on watches and clocks here than on cameras and optical goods. An enormous variety of makes and models are on sale. Be sure to get the manufacturer's guarantee stamped or signed if you buy a watch.

ENTERTAINMENT

Day and night, the action goes on in this vibrant city. To help you choose a nightlife scene, pick up a copy of Hong Kong Tourist Authority's dining and entertainment guide for listings, or just simply wander through the maze of neon signs and take your pick. *Hong Kong Diary* published weekly by HKTA tells what's happening in the arts. *Hong Kong Life* is published by the *Hong Kong Standard* on Sunday, and the *South China Morning Post* has an entertainment section on Friday.

Culture buffs are well catered to, and there is always a varied program of events, ranging from world-class concerts to local amateur dramatic productions.

A highlight of the arts calendar is the annual **Hong Kong Arts Festival,** a three-week dose of international culture in February, with concerts, recitals, plays, jazz, Chinese opera, and innovative productions put on by leading talent from both East and West. Tickets for the shows must be reserved well in advance. The **Festival of Asian Arts** takes place every other October, bringing to Hong Kong for two weeks orchestras, dance groups, opera, and drama companies from all over Asia.

There are more than 30 cinemas in Hong Kong, and the latest Western releases are shown in some of the larger ones. English-language films have Chinese subtitles. Films with

Mandarin dialogue also have Chinese subtitles, for the benefit of Cantonese speakers, and sometimes subtitles in English.

The **Hong Kong International Film Festival** takes place in April. More than 200 films from all over the world are shown at this two-week event. Ask at City Hall center about advance reservations.

The Performing Arts

Performance Venues. The theaters in the **Hong Kong Cultural Center** in Tsim Sha Tsui are the main venues for concerts and opera. Other performance centers are the **City Hall cultural complex,** with exhibition halls and theaters that present concerts, plays, and films; the **Hong Kong Academy for the Performing Arts** with two major theaters for dance, drama, and concert performances; and the **Hong Kong Arts Centre** in Wan Chai, where both local and visiting groups perform. Other centers for concerts, plays, and entertainment are Sha Tin Town Hall and Tsuen Wan Town Hall in the New Territories. Larger arenas, including the Queen Elizabeth Stadium, the Hong Kong Coliseum, and the Ko Shan Theater in Kowloon play host to various concerts, pop concerts, sporting events, and variety shows.

Traditional dance often takes to the streets during festivals in Hong Kong.

Classical Music. The Hong Kong Chinese Orchestra performs new and traditional works; a wide assortment of traditional and Chinese instruments are featured. The Hong Kong Philharmonic Orchestra was founded in 1975. Under its conductor, David Atherton, it offers Western classical works and new works by Chinese composers in a September-to-June season.

Chinese Opera. Cantonese opera is alive and well in Hong Kong, and the two other forms, Beijing and Kun, are sometimes presented. To most foreigners, this unique art form is likely to be inscrutable at first exposure, but everyone can appreciate the spectacle and the elaborate, glittering costumes. Although the music may seem strange to the unaccustomed ear, it certainly won't put you to sleep; cymbals and drums guarantee your alertness.

Dance. Hong Kong's three professional dance companies—the Hong Kong Ballet Company, the Hong Kong Dance Company, and the newer City Contemporary Dance Company—perform regularly, often at the Hong Kong Academy for the Performing Arts.

Theater. The two leading local troupes, the Chung Ying Theatre Company and the Hong Kong Repertory Theatre, perform in Cantonese; there are English-language performances at the Fringe Club theaters, 2 Lower Albert Road, in Central.

Hong Kong is graced with three accomplished professional companies to please dance afficionados.

Puppet Shows. The classic Chinese puppet is the shadow puppet, manipulated behind a screen by three rods, but hand puppet and marionette shows are also on offer, often for free at public parks and playgrounds.

Nightlife

Hong Kong by night can suit any taste—riotous, sedate, raw, or cultured. Note that sometimes there is a cover charge of HK$50 to HK$200 at clubs, which may or may not include a couple of drinks.

There are nightclubs in the principal hotels, with bands, dancing, and floor shows. Many restaurants and bars have live music.

Puppet shows often emulate the styles of Chinese Opera. These opera performers have the look of marionettes.

Jazz fans will find live jazz presented by international artists at the Jazz Club and Bar, 2/F, 34-36 D'Agular, Central; and at the Blue Note in the Kowloon Shangri-La Hotel in Tsim Sha Tsui. The Fringe Club, 21 Lower Albert Road, Central, is Hong Kong's best-known alternate entertainment venue, with jazz, rock, and other live music, in addition to a gallery for visual arts.

Bars with views and live music include Sky Lounge in the Sheraton Hotel and Towers, Tsim Sha Tsui; and Cyrano in

Calendar of Festivals

For the most up-to-date information, consult the Hong Kong Tourist Authority, or pick up a free copy of the HKTA's *Hong Kong Diary*. Note that precise dates cannot be given as Chinese festivals are fixed according to the lunar calendar.

January/February: *Lunar New Year.* Everything in Hong Kong, even business, shuts down for three days. This festival is family-oriented, a time for paying debts, dressing up, and giving gifts. The dominant motif for the holiday is flowers. People visit temples and hand out *lai see* (lucky money) packets to children and unmarried friends, accompanied by the words "Kung hei fat cho" ("May you prosper in the New Year"). There is a parade on the waterfront, and an elaborate fireworks display lights up the harbor.

February: *Spring Lantern Festival (Yuen Siu).* The last day of the Chinese New Year celebrations is also known as Chinese Valentine's Day, since it was traditionally the time when unmarried women donned their finest clothes and ventured out with their chaperones to meet some eligible young men.

April: *Ching Ming Festival.* This Confucian festival, timed to the solar calendar, is one of two annual holidays on which to honor the dead. Ancestors' graves are swept and offerings of food, wine, or flowers are made, while gold and silver "money" is burned to give the ancestors enough to spend in the afterworld.

April/May: *Birthday of Tin Hau.* The Taoist Goddess of the Sea is honored by fisherfolk with prayers for safe voyages and good catches. The liveliest celebration is at Joss House Bay, where decorated junks and sampans converge with offerings. Spectators can reach the beach by special excursion boats. Smaller-scale celebrations, including lion-dancing, take place at other Tin Hau temples, notably at Aberdeen.

May: *Birthday of the Lord Buddha.* In Buddhist temples throughout the territory, the Buddha's image is bathed in scented water to symbolize the washing away of sins. *Cheung Chau Bun Festival.* The small island of Cheung Chau celebrates its thanksgiving holiday over seven days. Towers are made of sticky buns; processions, lion and dragon dances, and traditional rites at the Pak Tai Temple give the island a carnival atmosphere.

May/June: *Dragon Boat Festival (Tuen Ng).* Oarsmen in long, thin dragon boats race to the beat of big bass drums and Chinese gongs. Annual International Dragon Boat races are usually held a few days after the festival in June or July.

July: *Birthday of Lu Pan.* The Taoist patron saint of carpenters and builders is honored with celebratory banquets.

August: *Seven Sisters' (Maidens') Festival.* A festival for lovers, centered on an old legend. Women praying for husbands leave offerings at Lovers' Rock. *Hungry Ghosts Festival (Yue Lan):* Paper offerings are burned and food left out to placate ghosts who have been temporarily released from the underworld.

September: *Mid-Autumn Festival.* Celebrating the year's harvest, this one is a children's favorite. As the full moon rises, tots carrying paper lanterns of traditional or space-age design congregate in open places or high places to admire the poetic sight. They eat moon cakes (ground sesame and lotus seeds or dates, perhaps enriched with duck egg) and take full advantage of being allowed to stay up late.

October: *Cheung Yeung Festival.* Nineteen centuries ago, so it is said, a man visited the hills on the advice of a fortune-teller. When he returned he found he was the sole survivor of a calamity. On the ninth day of the ninth moon, people visit the hillside graves of their ancestors and try to reach some high place for luck.

Tai Chi is a morning ritual for many Chinese. Lessons for visitors may be arranged.

the Island Shangri-La in Pacific Place. Pubs are numerous. In Tsim Sha Tsui, Ned Kelly's Last Stand on Ashley Road is an Aussie institution; Delaney's, 71-77 Peking Road, is one of Hong Kong's enduring Irish pubs.

The clubs and bars of Wan Chai, long the center of seedy nightlife, have become almost respectable. Joe Bananas, 23 Luard Road, is a Wan Chai mainstay for all-night partying. Rick's Cafe, 78-82 Jaffe Road, is a long-time disco that's still popular. A lot of the raunchy action has moved across the harbor to Tsim Sha Tsui East; this is also where you'll find pricey hostess clubs, popular with Japanese tourists, but definitely not for those on a budget.

Today's trendy spot is Soho (SOuth of HOllywood) around Hollywood Road, Elgin, and Stauton streets. Soho, along with the Lan Kwai Fong area, is popular with chuppies (Hong Kong yuppies) and has a lively bar scene. Causeway Bay also has a variety of bars and clubs. TOTT's, in the Excelsior Hotel, is a restaurant with live music and dancing and a harbor view.

Japanese karaoke bars have now become extremely popular with the locals. There are a number of these on Chatham Road South and around Cameron Street in Tsim Sha Tsui.

Nightlife tours are offered by a number of companies. The most typical of these are harbor cruises, usually including dinner and dancing on board an air-conditioned floating nightclub. There are evening bus tours that include visits to a restaurant and night spots; some tours combine a Chinese banquet with a visit to an open-air market and the panorama from Victoria Peak.

SPORTS

Participant Sports

Beaches. In subtropical Hong Kong you can swim from April to early November. There are more than 40 beaches in Hong Kong that are free to the public. Most have lifeguards on duty from April to October, changing rooms, toilets, and snack stands. On Hong Kong Island, Repulse Bay is the most popular; others are Shek O on the east coast and Stanley and Deep Water Bay on the south coast. They are very crowded, especially on summer

The abundant waters around Hong Kong are suited for competition, as well as transportation.

The Sha Tin Racecourse can accommodate over 80,000 bettors and spectators.

weekends. On the outlying islands, Cheung Chau and Cheung Sha are on Lantau, and Hung Shing Ye and Lo So Shing on Lamma; inquire about water pollution levels.

Golf. The Hong Kong Golf Club (Tel. 2812 7070) welcomes visitors to its three 18-hole courses at Fanling in the New Territories, or the 9-hole course at Deep Water Bay. The Discovery Bay Golf Club on Lantau island (Tel. 2987 7273) has an 18-hole Robert Trent Jones Jr. course, open to visitors Monday, Tuesday, and Friday. Many Hong Kong residents and visitors take the express train to Guangzhou to play at the Guangzhou Luhu Golf and Country Club (Tel. 2317 1933 in Hong Kong or 020-8350 7777). The 72-par course was designed by Dave Thomas.

Hiking. In the New Territories the famous MacLehose Trail stretches 97 km (60 miles) from Sai Kung Peninsula to Tuen Mun. The Lantau Trail is a 69-km (43-mile) circular trail on Lantau Island that begins and ends at Silvermine Bay. Both trails are divided into smaller segments of varying difficulty. Maps of hiking trails are available at the Government Publications Center, Low Block, Government Offices, 66 Queensway in Central. HKTA also has trail maps and sponsors the Guided Nature Walks, led by rangers, that include hikes in all the different regions of Hong Kong.

Jogging. Victoria Park has a jogging track in Causeway Bay.

Sailing. Because of the heavy harbor traffic, only sailors licensed by the Hong Kong authorities can run pleasure boats in local waters. Contact the Hong Kong Yacht Club at Tel. 2832 2817 for information.

Taijiquan (Tai Chi). HKTA offers lessons in these exercises that improve concentration and balance at Garden Plaza, Hong Kong Park, Admiralty (Tel. 2058 1234).

Tennis. There are 13 public courts at Victoria Park Tennis Centre (Tel. 2570 6168), near Tin Hau Station.

Spectator Sports

Horseracing. All levels of society share a feverish interest in the Sport of Kings. The racing schedule is September to June, and Hong Kong maintains two tracks—the older Happy Valley course on Hong Kong Island and the striking Sha Tin track in the New Territories. The Hong Kong Tourist Association runs a "Come Horseracing Tour," which includes entry to the Hong Kong Jockey Club visitors' box and members' enclosure, and a buffet-style meal.

> **The Macau International Fireworks Display Contest is the largest such contest in the world.**

Cricket. The Hong Kong International Cricket Series, held in late September, brings teams from all over the world.

Rugby. The Rugby Sevens sees teams come together from all over the world for 15 matches in March or early April.

CHILDREN'S HONG KONG

Hong Kong has many attractions that appeal to children of all ages. Hong Kong's many beaches are especially fun for children. Children love riding on Hong Kong's antique trams. A ride on the Peak Tram is sure to provide a thrill, and in the Peak Tower they'll enjoy the Peak Explorer ride and Ripley's Believe it or Not!

Ocean Park (see page 32) is popular with children of all ages. There's a special Kid's World that those under 12 can enter free when accompanied by a paying adult. The more daring can try out the terrifying roller-coaster rides.

Hong Kong's state-of-the-art interactive museums will interest children of all ages. The Science Museum in Tsim Sha Tsui East allows children to get their hands on over half of its 500 exhibits, while the nearby Space Museum has regular screenings on an enormous Omnimax screen in its Space Theater, making the night sky come vibrantly alive.

For children who love boats, riding the Star Ferry or ferry trips to outlying islands will be exciting, and the Dolphin Watch trip (see page 113) is certain to appeal. If you plan to visit during May, the carnival atmosphere of the Cheung Chau Bun Festival, with its high bamboo-and-paper towers covered in sticky buns, will fascinate the young ones.

With so much coastline on Hong Kong and its surrounding islands, the beach is bound to figure into your plans.

EATING OUT

The Chinese care about food with a passion only the French can rival. For the Chinese, eating is a pleasure imbued with philosophical profundities: even the dead are offered food and wine to make their journey from this life more peaceful.

The common Cantonese greeting is *"Nei sik jo fan mai a?"* — ("Have you had your rice yet?"). Chinese restaurants are a place for social gatherings. Eating out is one of the main forms of socializing, and the Chinese usually eat in large groups. The food is best enjoyed if there is a variety of dishes. If Chinese hosts invite you to a restaurant, put yourself in their hands; they will try to order according to their impression of your tastes.

Chefs have a demanding clientele. Chinese gourmets demand the freshest food from local farms and the sea—they require not only the best flavors but color, texture, and presentation to enhance the pleasure of the food. A proper Chinese meal is orchestrated, and must contain a harmonious progression from sweet to sour, crunchy to tender. A Chinese banquet is a triumph of the well-rounded art of food.

You rarely find a bad Chinese meal here. The big problem is how to choose from among the thousands of restaurants, and then among the hundreds of items on the menu. Let the waiter help you to choose just the right amount of food with the best range of tastes and textures.

In Hong Kong you'll find restaurants offering cuisines from all over Asia, and a wide choice of Western cuisines, especially French but also Italian, Dutch, and Mexican, and even steak, pizza, and kosher food. Vegetarians do not have an easy time in Hong Kong. Most Chinese chefs use chicken or other meat stock routinely in otherwise vegetarian dishes, but there are a handful devoted to a purely vegetarian cuisine.

MEAL TIMES

Most hotels serve a breakfast buffet of Chinese and Western food from about 7 to 10am. At lunchtime business people pack the restaurants from 1 to 2:30pm. Dinner is between 7:30 and 9:30pm, but Chinese restaurants are flexible; many are open from early in the morning until midnight without a break.

A traditional Chinese breakfast consists of *congee*, a rice gruel or porridge to which almost anything may be added. At back-street breakfast stalls you'll also see the early risers digging into noodle soup with hunks of vegetable or pork.

REGIONAL CUISINES

Chinese food comes in half a dozen principal styles, all very different from one another. In Hong Kong every major school of Chinese cooking is represented; restaurants have inherited recipes and brilliant cooks from all parts of China.

Cantonese

For visitors, this is probably the most familiar Chinese cuisine, as so many Cantonese emigrated, opened restaurants, and introduced new tastes to diners in the West. Cantonese food is either steamed or stir-fried, cooking methods that capture the natural flavor of the ingredients as well as the color and vitamins. A vast range of ingredients is used, and the flavors are many and often delicately understated.

Garoupa, a meat-flavored, local fish comes steamed in the company of ginger, spring onions, and soy sauce, with a touch of garlic. Prawns come in a sauce of sugar, vinegar, soy, and ketchup, colored with the addition of crisp red and green peppers and pineapple chunks. Lemon chicken consists of fried chunks of tender chicken in a creamy sauce of sugared lemon juice and chicken broth. A hearty soup is crabmeat and corn soup; soup is usually served towards the end of the meal. Steamed white rice is normally served with a Cantonese meal.

Chiu Chow

This cuisine from the Swatow region of southeast China excels in novel seasonings and rich sauces. Chefs also pride themselves on their amazing vegetable carvings that are part of every Chiu Chow banquet. Before and after dinner you will be presented with tiny cups of a strong and bitter tea, known as Iron Buddha.

Two very expensive Chiu Chow delicacies are shark's fin and bird's nest. A typical dish is minced pigeon: The pigeon meat is minced and fried with herbs, and you eat it wrapped in lettuce leaves. In Chiu Chow restaurants *congee* (rice porridge) is often served instead of rice.

Beijing (Peking)

The Chinese emperors made Beijing the gourmet center of the country, and Hong Kong's Peking restaurants still present truly imperial banquets (ordered in advance) with everything from nuts to soup, in that order. Northern food tends to be richer than

Cantonese food is familiar to many Westerners, but you still might be surprised.

Chinese dining offers a wide variety of experiences, from humble street food to gourmet cuisine with a view.

Cantonese food. Don't miss the dramatic smashing of the clay around "beggar's chicken," or one of the world's most delicious eating experiences, Peking duck. The duck is honey-coated before roasting, and is cut at the table. The celebrants put chunks of the crisp skin and tender flesh, along with spring onions and a sweet sauce, onto delicate pancakes, which are then rolled up and devoured.

Wheat, not rice, is the staple food in northern China. Peking restaurants serve noodles and various kinds of bread. They also specialize in wonderful dumplings, stuffed with meat or vegetables and prepared by steaming or frying.

Shanghai

Shanghai restaurants also serve the delicious dish known as "beggar's chicken." According to legend, the inventor was a tramp who stole a chicken but had no way to cook it. After tossing in some salt and onion, he smeared the bird in mud, then roasted it in his fire. When the mud was baked dry and he smashed the coating—the feathers came off with the clay and all the juicy tenderness of the bird remained. The recipe has become more sophisticated as mushrooms, pickled cabbage, shredded pork, bamboo shoots, and wine are added to the stuffing.

Shanghai food is an amalgam of a number of Chinese cuisines from surrounding cities. It tends to be more diverse and complicated as well as more thoroughly cooked than, say, Cantonese. Chili peppers, garlic, and ginger are used in moderation. Freshwater hairy crab, imported from Shanghai in autumn, steamed and eaten with the hands, is a popular dish. Shanghai diners usually prefer noodles to rice.

Szechwan

This food from southwestern China has become popular in America. It produces such sharp, hot flavors that it first takes your breath away, then awakens your palate. Once the fiery shock of the garlic-enhanced peppers has subsided, you can distinguish the other many elements in unlikely coexistence —bitter, sweet, fruity, tart, and sour.

Smoked duck, Szechwan style, is marinated in rice wine, with ginger and an array of spices, then steamed before being smoked over a specially composed wood fire. Deep-fried beef with vegetables is a dish in which the meat and most of the other ingredients—carrots, celery, peppers, garlic—are shredded and slowly fried over a low flame.

All Chinese foods are pleasing to the eye, but there are some Szechwan foods that appeal to the ear. "Thunder" dishes are topped with crisp rice, which sizzles and pops on contact with the other ingredients.

Hakka

The name Hakka means "guest people," referring to their migration to this region from northern China many centuries ago. Hakka cuisine involves the use of simple ingredients, especially versatile bean curd. Look for an ingenious dish called salted chicken; a coating of salt contains and increases the flavors while the bird is being baked.

Dim Sum

Late breakfast or lunch can consist of tea and *dim sum*, the small snacks which add up to a delicious, filling meal. Servers wander from table to table chanting the Cantonese names of

> The famous "thousand-year eggs" are duck eggs buried in lime for 60 days, with a resulting cheese-like taste.

the foods contained in bamboo steamers on their trays or carts. Choose whatever looks interesting—from spring rolls, spare ribs, dumplings, and so on. Dozens of different delicacies are displayed: from *siu mai* (pork and shrimp dumplings), to *har gau* (delicate steamed shrimp dumplings), and *cha siu bau* (barbecued pork buns). When you ask for the bill, the waiter will compute it on the basis of the number of empty dishes on the table.

DRINKS

The Chinese having a dinner party at the table next to you are probably drinking Cognac with their meal. Hong Kong claims the world's highest per-capita consumption of brandy, possibly because of a vague belief that it has aphrodisiac qualities. European and Australian table wines are also available, but at prices ranging from the tolerable to the quite shocking.

Few visitors develop a taste for Chinese wines, despite their 4,000-year history. Some are too sweet, others too strong. Unlike the Chinese grape and rice wines, the wheat wines are notorious for their alcoholic power. Mou Tai is a breathtaking case in point.

The best choice for the visitor is beer. The locally brewed San Miguel is cheap and refreshing. Tsingtao beer from China has a hearty European taste. You'll also find a large selection of European beers.

The Chinese have been drinking tea for many centuries as a thirst-quencher, general reviver, and ceremonial beverage. Tea in China is drunk without sugar or milk, although English-style tea is available in hotels. It's well worth making the effort to learn to appreciate the many varieties of tea and their histories.

Rounding off the beverage list are familiar soft drinks and delicious tropical fruit juices. Most hotels serve excellent coffee at breakfast, and it is also available in snack bars (though the coffee in Starbuck's here is disappointing).

A breakfast chef begins the day for guests at the Harbour Plaza Hotel.

To Help You Order...

Have you a table?	**Yau mo toi ah?**
I'd like a/an/some...	**Ngor seung yiu...**
The bill, please.	**Mai dan, m goi.**

beer	**bei jau**	meat	**yuk**
chopsticks	**fai ji**	menu	**chan pye**
cup	**bui**	rice	**faan**
dessert	**tim bun**	soup	**tong**
fish	**yue**	tea	**cha**
fruit	**sang gwo**	water	**sui**
glass	**bor lay bui**	wine	**jau**

Try Chopsticks

You'll lose face—and fun—if you don't learn to use chopsticks to eat your food in Hong Kong. There's no reason to feel self-conscious—the Chinese are tolerant when it comes to table manners.

Begin by settling the bottom stick firmly at the conjunction of the thumb and forefinger, balancing it against the first joint of the ring finger. The second stick pivots around the fulcrum made by the tip of the thumb and the inside of the forefinger.

Remember not to lay your chopsticks across each other, and never place them across the rice bowl, but rest them on the holder provided or against a plate.

Forks and knives are supplied in most restaurants. If it's any consolation, many Chinese don't feel quite at home with them either.

Dim sum is a delicious weekend ritual enjoyed by families throughout Hong Kong.

...and Read the Menu

bean curd and crabmeat soup	蟹肉豆腐羹
bean curd with pork in pepper sauce	麻婆豆腐
diced chicken with walnuts	合桃雞丁
diced pork with cashew nuts	腰果肉丁
fried bamboo shoots and cabbage	干煸冬筍
fried eel with soya sauce	炒鱔糊
fried shrimps	清炒蝦仁
fried sliced pork with green pepper	青椒肉絲
mushrooms with vegetables	菜扒鮮菇
shredded chicken with green pepper	辣子雞丁
sliced beef with green pepper and bean sauce	豉椒牛肉
sliced chicken, abalone and prawn soup	三絲湯
sliced fish with brown sauce	紅燒魚片
stewed yellow fish	糟溜黃魚
sweet and sour pork	咕嚕肉
Tientsin cabbage and asparagus	雞油津白

HANDY TRAVEL TIPS

An A–Z Summary of Practical Information

A

ACCOMMODATIONS (See also RECOMMENDED HOTELS, page 127)
Most of Hong Kong's more than 35,000 hotel rooms are in luxury or first-class hotels, so finding moderately priced or budget accommodations is not always easy. Hong Kong's high seasons are October to early December and March and April. In other months, particularly in summer, prices may drop, and bonuses like upgrades, free airport transport, and discounts may be offered.

The price of a room in Hong Kong often depends upon its view. For the best rates, check with a travel agent or look for a package that offers hotel and airfare. Rooms tend to be small except in the most expensive places. High- and mid-range hotels are all members of the Hong Kong Tourist Association (HKTA); check for membership in this organization when booking an inexpensive lodging.

Advance reservations are essential for moderately priced hotels, and advisable for all others. For visitors arriving without reservations, the Hotel Reservation Centre at the airport can arrange a room at any of the hotels affiliated with the Hong Kong Hotels Association; the service is provided free of charge and the desk is open from 8am–midnight.

Hong Kong hotels include all the major international chains. Many of the more modest establishments offer services comparable to first-class hotels. Posted rates cover the room price only; a 10% service charge and a 5% government tax are added to the bill at check-out time.

AIRPORT
International flights land at the Chek Lap Kok Airport, just off Lantau Island.

Arriving. Immigration and customs checks are efficient in this modern airport. Beyond the baggage inspection area you will find a bank, money changers, the Hotel Reservation Centre desk, and the information counters of both the Hong Kong Tourist Association and the Macau Government Tourist Office where you can pick up information packages and maps. The Ground Transportation Centre is the place to go for information about transportation into the city, or for taxis and limousine service.

Hong Kong

Airport Express (AEL)(Tel. 2881 8888) This rail link is the quickest and most efficient way to get into the city. Trains run every 10 minutes from 5:50am–1am daily to Kowloon (20 minutes travel time) and Hong Kong Central (24 minutes) stations where there is free shuttle bus service to many hotels. Buy tickets from ticket-issuing machines.

Airport Shuttle Service. (Tel. 2377 0733) The deluxe bus runs every 30 minutes, 24 hours a day, door-to-door to all hotels; book at the Airport Service Counter in the arrivals hall.

Airbuses. (Tel. 2873 0818) The buses serve all major hotels. Take A21 to Kowloon, All and A12 to Hong Kong Island. Travel time is about an hour. Buy tickets at the Commercial Service Counter or have exact fare ready.

Limousines and Taxis. Major hotels operate their own limousine services; go to the Hotel Reservation Centre if you have a reservation, or look for the hotel pick-up counters. If you take a taxi, you should be charged only what the meter reads, plus tolls and a charge for each piece of luggage placed in the trunk.

Departure. Some airlines, including Cathay Pacific, United, and Singapore Airlines, allow you to check in for your return flight at either Hong Kong Central Station or Kowloon Station up to 24 hours before your departure. Boarding passes will be issued, and luggage transferred to the airport.

The Airport Shuttle Service and limousines can be booked through your hotel concierge. Allow extra time for heavy traffic during rush hour.

B

BUDGETING FOR YOUR TRIP

To give you an idea of what to expect, here are some average prices in Hong Kong dollars. However, remember that prices change, so they should be regarded as approximate.

Airport Transfer. Limousine from the airport to your hotel, about HK$400; taxis HK$270–$330, plus tolls and luggage; Airport Express HK$60–HK$ 70; Airport Shuttle HK$120; Airbus HK$20–HK$23.

Buses and trams. Buses HK$1–$32, trams HK$1.20 for adults, HK80¢ for children, minibuses HK$3–$10, maxicabs HK$1-$8, Peak Tram HK$14 (one way), HK$21 (round-trip) for adults, HK$4 (one way), HK$6 (round-trip) for children.

Car rental. A compact car costs around HK$750 a day. A car or limo with a driver costs around HK$135 an hour.

Ferries. Star Ferry HK$1.70-$2.20; island ferries HK$14-HK$31; Macau ferry HK$130-HK$247.

Hotels. Luxury hotels range upward from HK$2,500, top line hotels from HK$1,800; medium range hotels begin at around HK$950, and inexpensive hotels below HK$950. All add 10% service charge and 5% government tax.

MTR. Mass Transit Railway fares are HK$4–HK$26, depending on distance.

Meals and drinks. In a moderately priced restaurant: set lunch HK$80–$150, dinner HK$150–$350; the many buffets are good value.

Taxis. HK$15 for first 2 km (1.2 miles), HK$1.40 for each succeeding 200 m, HK$20 for journeys via Cross Harbour Tunnel or Eastern Harbour Crossing (to cover driver's return toll), and HK$5 for each piece of baggage.

Trains. KCR from Kowloon to the boundary with China, first class HK$54, ordinary class HK$27.

C

CAR RENTAL (See also DRIVING)

Driving in Hong Kong is not recommended. Traffic can be a nightmare, streets are narrow and crowded, and parking often nearly impossible. Hong Kong's public transportation is so good that driving is never as convenient as the MTR or a bus. Moreover, distances are short, and walking is often an easy option.

All international and many local rental agencies operate in Hong Kong offering both self-drive and chauffeur-driven cars. Japanese, European, and American models are available.

Hong Kong

Major credit cards are accepted. To rent a car, drivers must be over 25 and have held a valid license from their home country or an international license for two years.

CLIMATE

The best time to visit Hong Kong is in October or November, when the temperature and humidity drop and days are clear and sunny. From December until late February you'll find the air moderately cool with the humidity still low (around 73%). In spring the humidity and temperature start rising. March and April can be very pleasant, but from May to mid-September it's extremely hot and often wet, with most of the annual rainfall recorded during these months.

The following chart gives an idea of the average monthly temperatures in Hong Kong, and the number of rainy days per month:

	J	F	M	A	M	J	J	A	S	O	N	D
∞C	15	15	18	22	25	28	28	28	27	25	21	17
∞F	59	59	64	72	77	82	82	82	81	77	70	63
days of rain	6	8	11	12	16	21	19	17	14	8	6	5

CLOTHING

From May to September lightweight summer clothing is called for, and a raincoat and umbrella might come in handy. In restaurants and hotels, beware of the air-conditioning, which can reduce the temperature to freezing. From late September to early December shirtsleeves and sweaters are appropriate, while in winter — from late December to February — a wool suit and a warm jacket or light coat is advisable.

Informality is generally the rule in dress. For sightseeing and shopping, virtually any fashion is appropriate. Shorts and T-shirts are perfectly acceptable, but shorts and halter tops are out of place at the more upscale restaurants and in Chinese temples. You'll see people in formal business attire in Hong Kong's Central business district. Bring along comfortable shoes for the steep slopes of Hong Kong.

CRIME AND SAFETY (See also EMERGENCIES and POLICE)

Hong Kong is a safe city, night and day. The streets are usually full of people until late at night. As the signs in the trams warn you, "Beware of pickpockets." This applies to any crowded place, and Hong Kong has some of the most crowded places you've ever seen. Be especially careful in crowded markets such as the Temple Street Night Market, and on rush hour buses and MTR trains. It is best to leave your valuables in a hotel safe, including your passport.

However, you should be aware that there are some safety concerns in Macau. Although these are not likely to affect tourists, Macau has a recent history of gang warfare.

CUSTOMS AND ENTRY REQUIREMENTS

For most nationalities, only a passport is required for entry into Hong Kong. Subjects of the UK can stay up to six months without a visa; Canadians, Australians, and New Zealanders can stay for three months, and US citizens for one month.

To enter Macau, only a passport is needed, and most visitors can stay up to 20 days without a visa.

Visas are required for entry into the People's Republic of China, so if you are visiting Guangzhou, Shenzhen, or taking any other excursion over the border, you will need a visa. Short-term tours to China include visas; otherwise visas can be arranged at the office of China Travel Service (CITS), 27-33 Nathan Road, Tsim Sha Tsui.

You can bring into Hong Kong duty-free: 200 cigarettes or 50 cigars or 250 grams tobacco, and 1 liter spirits or 1 liter wine. Firearms are strictly controlled, and can only be brought in by special permit. There are no currency restrictions.

When returning home, duty-free quotas are as follows. Australia: A$400 worth of merchandise, 250 cigarettes or 250 grams tobacco, and 1 liter spirits or 1 liter wine. Canada: Can$500 worth of merchandise, 200 cigarettes, 400 grams tobacco, 50 cigars, 1.4 liters spirits, and 1.4 liter wine. New Zealand: NZ$700 worth of merchandise, 200 cigarettes or 50 cigars or 250 grams tobacco, and 1.1 liters spirits and 4.5 liters wine. UK: £145 worth of merchandise, 200 ciga-

Hong Kong

rettes or 50 cigars or 250 grams tobacco, and 1 liter spirits and 2 liters wine. US: US$400 worth of merchandise, 200 cigarettes and 100 cigars, 1 liter wine or spirits; Cuban cigars, plants or fresh food-stuffs are prohibited; antiques over 100 years old are duty-free.

D

DRIVING (see also CAR RENTAL)

Anyone over 18 with a valid license and third-party insurance can drive in Hong Kong for 12 months without having to pay for a local license. Drivers must carry a valid driver's license and photo identification at all times.

Road Conditions. Congestion is a serious problem in the city, sometimes leading to impatient, imprudent driving. Beware of inattentive pedestrians. Good highways connect to the New Territories and the airport.

Rules and Regulations. As in Britain and Australia, Hong Kong traffic keeps to the left. All passengers in private cars, front and back, are required to wear seatbelts. Drivers may not use hand-held mobile phones while driving. Note that across the border in China, as in Europe and the US, cars keep to the right. The speed limit is 30mph (50km/h) in towns, elsewhere as marked.

Parking. This can be a headache, especially in central areas, despite the multi-story parking garages. In busy streets, meters operate from 8am to midnight Monday–Saturday, and wardens are ever alert.

Breakdowns. Telephone the agency from which you rented the car. In an emergency, dial 999 for the police. The Automobile Association is at 391 Nathan Road, Yau Ma Tei; Tel. 2739 5273.

Road Signs. Most road signs in Hong Kong are the standard international pictographs.

The following words may help you in explaining your problems to non-English-speaking Chinese:

There's been an accident.	**Yau yi ngoi a.**
collision	**jong che**
flat tire	**tire baau tai**

E

ELECTRICITY

Standard voltage in Hong Kong is 220-volt, 50-cycle AC. Many hotels have razor fittings for all standard plugs and voltages. For other units, transformers and plug adapters will be needed; you may need a plug for your laptop even if it is equipped to deal with both 220 and 110 volts. Most hotels furnish hairdryers.

EMBASSIES AND CONSULATES

Consulates are generally open Monday–Friday, 9am–noon and 2–4 or 5pm. Various sections may be open at different hours; to make sure, telephone first.

Australia: 23rd–24th floors, Harbour Centre, 25 Harbour Road, Wan Chai; Tel. 2827 8881.

Canada: 12th–14th floors, Tower 1, Exchange Square, 8 Connaught Place, Central; Tel. 2810 4321.

New Zealand: 65th floor, Central Plaza, 18 Harbour Road, Wan Chai; Tel. 2525 5044.

UK:1 Supreme Court Road, Central; Tel. 2901 3000.

US: 26 Garden Road, Central; Tel. 2523 9011.

EMERGENCIES

Dial 999 for Police, Fire, or Ambulance departments. St. John's Ambulance Brigade is a free service; Tel. 2576 6555 on Hong Kong island, 2713 5555 in Kowloon, or 2639 2555 in the New Territories.

Hospitals with 24-hour emergency services are: Queen Mary Hospital, 102 Pokfulam Road, Hong Kong Island, Tel. 2855 4111; Queen Elizabeth Hospital, 30 Gascoigne Road, Kowloon; Tel. 2958 8888; and King Adventist Hospital, 40 Stubbs Road, Hong Kong Island; Tel. 2574 6211. Many hotels have doctors on call.

In Macau, dial Tel. 573333 for the police and Tel. 572222 for fire.

Help! **Gau meng ah!**

Police! **Geng tsa!**

G

GAY AND LESBIAN TRAVELERS

Hong Kong is still fairly conservative, despite a softening of anti-gay attitudes since the 1991 Crimes Ordinance that de-criminalized homosexual acts. Gays have been pushing for anti-discrimination laws. There's a gay scene around Glenealy and Wyndham streets in Central and along Jaffe Road in Wan Chai. The Web site for nightlife information is www.gaystation.com.hk. China's official attitude toward gays at present is ambivalent.

GETTING THERE

From North America. A number of airlines offer direct flights between hubs in North America and Hong Kong; only a few of these are nonstop. The official airline of Hong Kong is Cathay Pacific Airways (Tel. 800/233-2742 <www.cathaypacific.com>, with daily nonstop service from Los Angeles, Vancouver, and Toronto, and direct service, with a stop in Vancouver, from New York. Nonstop flights are also offered by Continental Airlines (Tel. 800/525-0280 <www.continental.com>) with daily flights from Newark, NJ; Canadian Airlines International (Tel.800/426-7000 <www.cdnair.ca>), with daily flights from Vancouver; Singapore Airlines (Tel. 800/742-3333 <singapore-air.com>) with daily service from San Francisco; and United Airlines (Tel. 800/241-6522; <www.united.com>), with daily nonstop service from JFK New York, Chicago, San Francisco, and Los Angeles.

Airlines with direct flights include Northwest Airlines (Tel. 800/225-2525 <www.nwa.com>), which also flies to Macau; Japan Airlines (Tel. 800/525-3663 japanair.com); Korean Air (Tel. 800/438-5000 <koreanair.com>). China Airlines (Tel. 800/227-5118; <www.china-airlines.com>) flies daily from New York with a change in Taipei.

From the UK. CathayPacific (Tel. 0171/747 8888), British Airways (Tel. 0845/773 3377 <www.britishairways.com>), and Virgin Atlantic Airways (Tel. 01293/747747 <www.virgin.com>) offer daily nonstop service from London to Hong Kong.

From Australia and New Zealand. Both Qantas (tel 131313 <www.qantas.com.au>) and Cathay Pacific (Tel. 131747) offer daily nonstop service from Sydney and Melbourne. From New Zealand, Cathay Pacific (Tel. 0508/800454) offers daily nonstop service from Auckland.

GUIDES AND TOURS

There are all kinds of organized tours in Hong Kong, from orientation tours of the city, night cruises of the harbor, and tours of the islands to trips farther afield to Macau, Shenzhen, and Guangzhou.

The Hong Kong Tourist Authority (HKTA) organizes a large assortment of tours. Tour operators include Gray Line Tours of Hong Kong Ltd., 5/F 72 Nathan Road, Tsim Sha Tsui (Tel. 2368 7111); Arrow Travel Agency Ltd. has a travel desk in the Kowloon Hotel lobby, 19-21 Nathan Road, Tsim Sha Tsui, that can book most tours; Watertours (Tel. 2739 3302) is the largest operator of boat and junk cruises; Splendid Tours and Travel Ltd. (Tel. 2316 2151) has night cruises among its offerings; and China Travel Service of Hong Kong Ltd. (CITS) runs 1–3-day tours of Guangzhou and other South China destinations.

Most interesting for the visitor who has a few days in Hong Kong are the theme tours sponsored by HKTA. Outstanding is the "Heritage Tour," which takes you to unique historic sites in the New Territories. "The Land Between Tour" takes you to traditional villages in the New Territories. The Feng Shui tour explores this traditional concept (see box, page 68).

Hong Kong Dolphinwatch Ltd., 1528 Star House, Tsim Sha Tsui (Tel. 2984 1414) has a half-day eco-cruise to sight Hong Kong's threatened pink dolphins.

If you are interested in hiring a guide for a group or a personal guide, contact HKTA in Hong Kong. Contact CITS for guides in other South China destinations.

H

HEALTH AND MEDICAL CARE (also see EMERGENCIES)

There are no special health precautions to take in Hong Kong. No vaccinations are needed. Food is safe everywhere, even in roadside stalls, and you can safely drink the water, though most people prefer bottled water. Avoid eating locally caught shellfish and oysters, and never eat them raw; most restaurants use imported or farmed varieties. Be aware that outside major hotels, MSG is widely used.

Traveling into China requires a few extra precautions. You should not drink the tap water; drink only bottled water and use bottled water to brush your teeth. However, the thermos of hot water supplied in all hotel rooms is perfectly safe to drink. It is also wise not to eat raw food in China; choose fruit that can be peeled.

During the hot, humid summer months, remember to limit exposure to the sun. Wear a hat and use a sunscreen. Always carry a bottle of water, especially when hiking.

The International Association for Medical Assistance to Travelers (IMAT) has a Web site <www.sentex.net/imat>.

a bottle of drinking water	**yat tchun sui**
I want to see a...	**Ngor yiu tai...**
doctor	**yee sang**
dentist	**nga yee**

HOLIDAYS

Thanks to the convergence of British and Chinese traditions, Hong Kong celebrates 17 holidays a year. Though the banks close, most businesses carry on as usual. The only holiday on which Hong Kong really shuts down is the Lunar New Year. Chinese holidays are fixed according to the lunar calendar, so exact dates cannot always be given.

January 1	New Year's Day
January or February	Lunar New Year (3–4 days)
March or April	Easter (Good Friday, Easter Monday)
April	Ching Ming Festival
May 1	Labor Day
May or June	Tuen Ng (Dragon Boat) Festival
July (first weekday)	Establishment Day of the Special Administrative Region
September	The day following the mid-Autumn Festival
October 1	National Day
October	Chung Yeung Festival

| December 25 | Christmas Day |
| December 26 | Boxing Day (day after Christmas) |

LANGUAGE

The official languages of Hong Kong are English and Chinese. It is not altogether clear whether "Chinese" means Mandarin (*putonghua*) or Cantonese, which is commonly spoken by the local residents. The expectation is that *putonghua,* the official language of China, will eventually become the official language here. For a discussion of language, see the box on page 15. Macau's official languages are Chinese and Portuguese, though few people today speak the latter.

The following approximations of Cantonese greetings may help you make contact with the locals:

Good morning	**jo san**
Good afternoon	**ng on**
Good evening	**mang on**
Good night	**jo tau**
Goodbye	**joy geen**
Please (for service)	**m goi**
Please (invitation)	**tcheng**
Thank you (for service)	**m goi**
Thank you (for a gift)	**dor jeh**

Here are some everyday Hong Kong words:

amah	housemaid
chop	seal or stamp on a document
fung shui	lucky siting of building or graves
gwailo	Europeans, foreigners
hong	big business firm
joss	luck
pak pai	illegal taxi
yam seng	"cheers," "bottoms up"

M

MEDIA

Newspapers and Magazines. Local English-language dailies are the *South China Morning Post,* and the *Hong Kong Standard;* the *China Daily* is a newspaper in English published in Beijing. The *Asian Wall Street Journal,* published Monday–Friday in Hong Kong, emphasizes business and financial coverage. The *International Herald Tribune,* edited in Paris, is printed simultaneously in Hong Kong six days a week. Newspapers and magazines from Europe, Asia, and the US are easily available at hotels and bookshops.

Radio and Television. Hong Kong has three TV channels in English and two in Chinese. The Chinese channels sometimes show foreign-language films which are dubbed into Cantonese; satellite and cable stations are becoming increasingly available. The "Star World" satellite station shows re-runs of US and British television programs.

There are six English-language radio channels providing a broad range of programs, from easy listening to news and current affairs. The BBC World Service also broadcasts 24 hours a day.

MONEY

Currency. Hong Kong's currency is freely convertible, and is pegged to the US dollar at a rate of around 7.8. The Hong Kong dollar is divided into 100 cents. Banknotes are circulated in denominations of HK$10 (being phased out), HK$20, HK$50, HK$100, HK$500, and HK$1,000. Banknotes are issued by three local banks, Hongkong and Shanghai Banking Corporation, the Bank of China, and the Standard Chartered Bank. Coins, however, are minted by the Hong Kong government; they come in denominations of 10, 20, and 50 cents and HK$1, HK$2, HK$5, and HK$10 (the coin replacing the HK$10 note). Note that the 10-cent and 50-cent pieces look confusingly alike. Britain's Queen Elizabeth, who once appeared on these coins, has been replaced by the flower of the bauhinia tree, Hong Kong's regional emblem.

Currency in Macau and China. In China, the renminbi (RMB) or yuan is not a convertible currency; you can change your Hong Kong dollars (or any other currency) to yuan, but it does not go the other way. However, Hong Kong dollars are accepted in both Guangzhou and Shenzhen. Macau's currency is the pataca, and the same rules apply. Both the yuan and the pataca have an exchange value roughly the equivalent of the Hong Kong dollar, i.e. you will be charged in Hong Kong dollars about what you would be charged if you were paying in patacas or yuan.

Currency Exchange. Foreign currencies can be exchanged at banks, hotels, money changers, and major shopping outlets. Banks have better exchange rates, but charge a commission. Licensed money changers charge no commission, but the rates offered are about equivalent to a 5% commission. Money changers are found in all tourist areas and are open on holidays and late into the evening.

ATMs. ATMs are found all over Hong Kong, and banks do not usually charge a fee for the service. There are ATMs in Guangzhou and Shenzhen; but these are harder to find.

Credit Cards. Credit cards and charge cards are accepted everywhere you go in Hong Kong. Major hotels, restaurants, and shops in China also accept the well-known credit cards.

Traveler's Checks. Traveler's checks are widely accepted in shops, though you'll probably get a better exchange rate at a bank. You must show your passport when you cash a check. They are particularly useful in China, where a convenient ATM may not be available.

OPEN HOURS

Most government offices are open 9am–1pm and 2–5pm Monday–Friday, and 9am–1pm Saturday.

Banking hours are usually 9am–4:30pm Monday–Friday, and 9am–12:30pm Saturday. Some banks stop transactions an hour before closing time.

Hong Kong

Business offices are normally open Monday–Friday 9am–5pm, closed for lunch 1–2pm; Saturday 9am–5pm. Post offices are open Monday–Friday 9:30am–5pm and Saturday until 1pm.

Most shops are open seven days a week. Shops on Hong Kong Island are open 10am–6pm in Central, 10am–9:30 pm in Causeway Bay and Wan Chai, and 10am–9:30pm or later in Tsim Sha Tsui.

Museums are open from 10 or 11am–6pm. Most close one day a week, and all close on public holidays.

P

POLICE

The Hong Kong Police Force is one of the world's best equipped, with computerized and radio-controlled forces. The Force deals not only with crime and traffic but also has coast guard duties. Living up to Hong Kong's reputation as a fashion center, the police dress in smart, trimly tailored uniforms. Those with a red label under their shoulder badges speak English, but all police are to some extent bilingual.

Where's the police station, please?	**Tsai goon hai bean doe m goi?**

POST OFFICES

The main post office is on Hong Kong Island at 2 Connaught Place, just to the west of the Star Ferry terminal. There is a philatelic center on the ground floor; mailing and stamps are taken care of on the first floor. In Kowloon, post offices are located at 405 Nathan Road, between the Jordan and Yau Ma Tei subway stations, and at 10 Middle Road, one block north of Salisbury Road. For information, call Tel 2921 2222.

Post offices in Hong Kong deal only with mailing letters and packages. For faxing, telex, and other services, see the business center in your hotel.

PUBLIC TRANSPORTATION

Hong Kong's public transport system is one of the most efficient and easy to use anywhere; it's also remarkably inexpensive. Be aware that buses, ferries, and trams require the exact fare, so it is wise to carry some small change. The Octopus Card, which can be purchased at MTR stations, is a convenient electronic card accepted on most buses and ferries, the MTR system, trams, trains in the New Territories, and the Airport Express Line. It costs HK$150 (including an HK$50 refundable deposit), and can be reloaded in HK$100 units.

MTR. Hong Kong's Mass Transit Railway is one of the world's most modern, attractive, and easy-to-use subways. It operates daily 6am–1am, and connects Kowloon, Hong Kong Island and the New Territories. The four lines are color-coded; signs and train announcements are in both English and Cantonese. Tickets for single fares, ranging from HK$4–HK$26 depending on distance, can be purchased from vending machines. Be sure to take your ticket when it pops up on the turnstile; you will need it to exit when you reach your destination.

Ferries. The Star Ferry is not just a means of transportation, but a not-to-be missed visitor experience. The ferry connects Tsim Sha Tsui with Hong Kong Island at Central, and runs daily 6:30am–11:30pm every three to five minutes, and costs HK$1.70 for ordinary class and HK$2.20 for first class on the upper deck.

There are many other ferries connecting sections of the city: From Central to Hung Hom (near the KCR Railway Station); from Wan Chai to Tsim Sha Tsui and Hung Hom; and hoverferry service between Central and Tsim Sha Tsui East.

Ferries to the outlying islands are operated by the Hong Kong & Yumati Ferry Company Ltd. (HKF; Tel. 2542 3081). Most depart from the Outlying Island Ferry Piers west of the Star Ferry terminus on Central. Fares vary, with the highest being HK$3l. Jetfoils and catamarans to Macau leave from the Macau Ferry Terminal, just west of the Star Ferry about every 15 minutes 7am–5:30pm and every hour 6pm–6am; one-way fares are HK$130–HK$247, slightly more on weekends.

Buses. The bus service in Hong Kong is good and relatively cheap. Double-decker buses run 6am–midnight and cover even remote parts of Hong Kong. Fares range from HK$1.20–HK$45, depending on distance, and exact fare must be deposited in the box next to the driver as you get on. There are three bus companies: New World First Bus (Tel. 2136 888), Kowloon Motor Bus (KMB; Tel. 2745 4466), and Citybus (Tel. 2873 0818). Major bus terminals are located on both sides of the Star Ferry, and on Hong Kong Island at Exchange Square. Most bus stops are marked by a disc saying "all buses stop here."

"Public Light Buses" seat 16 passengers. You can hail them everywhere and get off almost anywhere along their route. Tell the driver when you want to get off and pay as you leave. Minibuses marked with a green stripe go to the Mid Levels, up to the Peak, and to Aberdeen. You can find them in Central and along Nathan Road. Minibuses marked with a red stripe have routes around West Point, Central, Causeway Bay, Quarry Bay, and Shau Kei Wan. Some of them also go over to Kowloon, and these minibuses can be hailed in Causeway Bay or Wan Chai.

Maxicabs are distinctive green-and-yellow vehicles that run to set routes with fixed fares ranging from HK$2–HK$22; pay as you get on. The destination is indicated by a sign at the front, but they may be hard to read, or be only in Chinese.

Trams. Hong Kong's picturesque double-decker trams are also a tourist attraction and provide a pleasant way to see the sights. Slow but sure, they traverse the north coast of Hong Kong Island between Kennedy Town and Shau Kei Wan. Pick one up on Des Voeux, Queensway, or Hennessy roads. Enter at the rear and exit at the front, dropping HK$2 into the fare box as you leave. It's a flat rate regardless of the distance traveled. The service operates between 6am and 1am.

Trains. The Kowloon-Canton Railway (KCR) runs 21 miles (34km) from Hung Hom in Kowloon to the border of China, and the local trains that serve commuters in the New Territories are an excellent way of visiting some of the towns and villages of the New Territories. Generally trains run daily every 3–10 minutes. Fares are very reasonable, costing HK$9 for ordinary class to Sheung Shui and HK$18 for first class.

There is also a Light Rail Transit system (LRT) that operates in the northwestern part of the New Territories linking the towns of Tuen Mun and Yuen Long. Trains run from 5:30am until 12:30am during the week and 6am–midnight on Sundays and public holidays.

Taxis. Hong Kong's metered taxis can be hailed on the street except in some restricted areas. Taxis on Hong Kong Island and Kowloon are red. Fares start at HK$15 for the first 2km, and go up HK$1.40 for every 200 meters; there are extra charges for luggage (HK$5 per piece) and trips through tunnels (HK$20 for the Cross-Harbour Tunnel). Be warned that taxi drivers often don't speak English, so it's a good idea to have your destination and the name of your hotel written in Chinese. Many hotels print a list of well-known places in Chinese characters and English that you can carry with you to show to your driver.

Funicular. The modernized Peak Tram funicular railway links Garden Road with Victoria Peak. The climb straight up the mountainside to the Peak Tower takes a breathtaking eight minutes; from the top there's a panoramic view. The tram costs HK$30 and runs daily 7am–midnight every 10 minutes or so.

R

RELIGION

Confucianism, Buddhism, and Taoism or a mixture thereof are the major religions in Hong Kong. There are also Christian churches of every denomination, Islamic mosques, Hindu temples, and Jewish and Baha'i houses of worship.

Visitors will find Anglican/Episcopal services at St. John's Cathedral in Central on Hong Kong Island, and at St. Andrew's Church on Nathan Road in Kowloon. Catholic masses are held at Rosary Chapel on South Chatham Road in Kowloon. For information about services, see the Saturday issue of the South China Morning Post, which runs announcements from churches.

Kowloon Mosque (Jamia Masjid) catering to Hong Kong's sizable Muslim population is beside Kowloon Park, on Nathan Road.

T

TELEPHONE

Hong Kong's country code is 852; Macau's country code is 853, and both places have 8-digit telephone numbers. The telephone system in Hong Kong is excellent for both local and international calls, and you can expect a clear connection.

Subscribers in Hong Kong pay a flat fee, and are not charged for local calls, so if you want to make a local call, you can walk into any shop and ask to use the phone. Some shops keep their phone on the front counter. Public phones require a HK$1 coin or a phone card. Phone cards, available at 7-Eleven stores and Hong Kong Telephone's retail shops, have values of HK$25, HK$50, and HK$100. Hotels usually tack a surcharge on both local and international calls.

For an English-speaking information service dial 1081; if you have difficulty in getting a number, dial 109. International direct-dial calls can be made at Hong Kong Telecom International, Shop 116, Princes Building, Des Voeux Road, Central. For overseas calls dial 001 (10011 for collect/reverse charge calls).

TIME ZONES

Before you make any overseas telephone calls, have a look at the following chart, so you won't wake someone halfway round the world.

The hours refer to the months when many countries in the northern hemisphere move their clocks one hour ahead (Daylight Savings Time). Hong Kong stays the same year-round, at GMT + 8.

New York	London	HongKong	Sydney	Auckland
7am	noon	7pm	9pm	11pm

TIPPING

Tipping in Hong Kong is somewhat confusing; tipping was never customary in China, although the British introduced it to Hong Kong. Who should be tipped and when is not always clear, especially inside China. Most hotels and restaurants routinely add a 10% service charge, but in upscale establishments, an extra 5–10% may be expected; in inexpensive places, round up the bill or leave up to 5%.

Unlike in Europe, tourist guides do not indicate that they expect a tip; however, they should receive about 10% of the cost of the tour. A hotel porter should receive HK$5–HK$10 per bag; an airport porter about HK$2. Hotel room attendants should get about 2% of the bill, but this is not obligatory. Lavatory attendents expect HK$2–HK$5, depending on the establishment. Tip hairdressers/barbers 10–15%. Tipping taxi and limo drivers is optional; you can simply round up the fare.

The best rule is to tip according to how you feel about the situation; anything you give will be graciously received.

TOILETS

Toilets are not easy to find in Hong Kong. The best bets are shopping malls, hotels, and restaurants where you have eaten a meal or snack, or fast food places. Places frequented by tourists and upscale establishments will have Western toilets, both in Hong Kong, Guangzhou, and on the islands. But you can encounter Chinese toilets in non-tourist areas or even in restaurants with a largely Chinese clientele; most of these in Hong Kong are clean and well-maintained. Toilet paper is not always provided, so it is wise to carry your own. To use the Chinese toilet, face the hood; be sure you put your used toilet paper in the wastebasket.

Where are the toilets?   **Chi saw hai bean doe?**

TOURIST INFORMATION

The Hong Kong Tourist Authority (HKTA) operates information and gift centers at key areas for visitors; the first one you'll encounter is the counter in the arrival hall at Chek Lap Kok, open daily 7am–11pm. The main office is at 99 Queens Road in Central, open daily 8am–6pm. On the Kowloon side in Tsim Sha Tsui, an office is on the Star Ferry Concourse, open the same hours. The HKTA Visitor Hotline, Tel. 2508 1234, operates daily 8am–6pm.

The HKTA publishes free brochures and literature about various aspects of Hong Kong; the "Official Hong Kong Guide" is a monthly information booklet with an overview of Hong Kong's attractions, shopping tips, and current events and exhibits. Free maps are available.

Hong Kong

Several weekly and monthly publications, free at restaurants and other outlets, tell you what's going on. *Hong Kong Diary* is a weekly publication; others are *BC* and "Hong Kong Life," a supplement of the newspaper, *Hong Kong Standard*. The *South China Morning Post* publishes an entertainment section on Friday. The monthly publication, *Where,* free at HKTA offices, tells you what's going on in Hong Kong. *The South China Morning Post* has an entertainment section Friday.

There is also a counter for the Macau Government Tourist Office (MTGO) (Tel. 2769 7970) at Chek Lap Kok, open daily 9am–10:30pm (closed for lunch and dinner). MTGO offices are at both ends of the Macau ferry terminal: Room 336, 3/F, on the departure floor in Hong Kong, and in the arrival hall at the Macau Ferry Terminal. Maps of Macau are available as well as the publication *Macau Travel Talk* and the pamphlet "Macau Walking Tours."

Overseas you can contact HKTA branch offices. Australia: Hong Kong House, Level 4, 80 Druitt Street, Sydney, NSW 2000; tel. (02) 9283 3083. Canada: Hong Kong Trade Centre, 9 Temperance Street, Toronto, Ontario M5H 1Y6; Tel. (416)366-2389. New Zealand: PO Box 2120, Auckland; tel. (09) 307 2580. UK: 6 Grafton St. London WIX 3LB; tel. (0171)533-7100. US: 115 E. 54th St, New York, NY 10022, Tel. (212)421-3382; 401 N. Michigan Ave. Suite 1640, Chicago IL 60611, Tel (312)329-1828; 10940 Wilshire Blvd, Suite 2050, Los Angeles CA 90024, Tel. (310)208-4582.

TRAVELERS WITH DISABILITIES

Hong Kong is not an easy place for travelers with disabilities. Hong Kong's frequent steps and its many steep streets, narrow crowded footpaths, and the pedestrian overpasses on Hong Kong Island are not easily negotiated. However, some hotels have special facilities for the disabled, most buildings have elevators, escalators are common, and taxis are inexpensive and easy to find. Contact HKTA for information on accommodations and advice on services catering to visitors with special needs. The Society for Advancement of Travel for the Handicapped (SATH) has a Web site <www.sath.org>.

WEB SITES

HKTA's Web sites are <www.discoverhongkong.com> and <www.hkta.org>. For lifestyle information, try <www.totallyhk.com>. The *South China Morning Post* has a site, <www.scmp.com.hk>. The Web site for the Hong Kong Arts Festival, which takes place in February, is <www.artsfestival.org>. Macau's tourist information Web site is <www.macautourism.gov.mo>. An excellent site for finding the best deal on airfares and booking flights and hotel accommodations is <www.travelocity.com>. For airfares try <www.bestfares.com>.

Many hotels offer internet access. If yours doesn't, there are cyber-cafés all over Hong Kong. Pacific Coffee Company is on 1/F, International Finance Center, 1 Harbour View Street (Tel. 2868 5100); i-Cable Station, 2/F is in Ocean Terminal, Harbour City, Tsim Sha Tsui.

WEIGHTS AND MEASURES

The international metric system is in official use. However, Chinese measures are still commonly used. Food products are generally sold by the catty (1.3lb s/600 g). Other items are measured by the *tael* (1.3oz/38g), and the chin (1.10lb/300 g). For length, the *tsün* (1.5in/37mm) and *check* (1.2ft/37cm) are used in markets.

Length

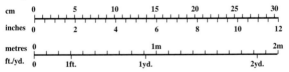

Weight

Hong Kong

Temperature

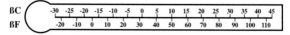

Fluid measures

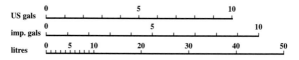

Distance

Y

YOUTH HOSTELS

Hong Kong's youth hostels are located in remote scenic areas, but are easily accessible by public transport. The main hostels are Ma Wui Hall, top of Mt. Davis Path, Mt. Davis, Western District (Tel. 2817 5715); and Bradbury Lodge, 66 Ting Kok Road, Tai Mei Tuk Tai Po, New Territories (Tel. 2662 5123). For information, contact the Youth Hostels Association, Tel. 2788 1638.

More centrally located budget establishments with simple or bunk-bed rooms include the BP International House, 8 Austin Road, Tsim Sha Tsui (Tel. 2376 1333); Booth Lodge, run by the Salvation Army, 11 Wing Sing Lane, Yau Ma Tei, (Tel 2771 9266); and Garden View International House, overlooking the Zoo at 1 MacDonnell Road, Central (Tel. 2877 3737).

Recommended Hotels

Hong Kong has some of the most luxurious hotels in the world, with representatives from all the major international chains. Hotels listed below have full air-conditioning, offer 24-hour or limited room service, and a wide range of facilities. Hong Kong hotels have excellent business services and conference facilities; many have shopping malls.

Reservations are strongly recommended, particularly in summer and at Christmas. If you do arrive without making advance arrangements, the Hong Kong Hotel Reservation Center at the International Airport will be happy to arrange accommodations for you on your arrival.

As a basic guide, the symbols below have been used to indicate high-season rates in Hong Kong dollars, based on double occupancy, with bath or shower. Unless otherwise noted, hotels take all major credit cards. A 10% service charge and 5% government tax will be added to the bill.

$$$$	above HK$2,500
$$$	HK$1,600 to HK$2,500
$$	HK$950 to HK$1,600
$	below HK$950

CENTRAL

Conrad International Hong Kong $$$$ *Pacific Place, 88 Queensway; Tel. 2521 3838; Fax 2521 3888; <www.conrad.com.hk>*. A modern hotel set above Pacific Place with good views over the city. Rooms have classic furnishings with wood paneling and polished granite; all have voice mail, fax machines, and dataports. Nicolini's is a fine Italian restaurant; there are also Cantonese, French, and international restaurants. Business center and conference facilities, health center, outdoor swimming pool. 513 rooms.

Island Shangri-La Hong Kong $$$$ *Pacific Place, Supreme Court Road; Tel. 2877 3838; Fax 2521 8742; <www.shangri-la.com>.* The outstanding feature here is a 17-story atrium with abundant greenery. Large rooms with oversize bathrooms have dataports and views of the harbor or Victoria Peak. Continental, Cantonese, and Japanese restaurants. Conference facilities and business center, outdoor swimming pool, jogging track, and health center. 565 rooms.

Mandarin Oriental $$$$ *5 Connaught Road; Tel. 2522 0111; Fax 2810 6190; <www.mandarin-oriental.com>.* Located in the heart of the business district, this landmark hotel is rated as one of the top hotels of the world. Most of the spacious rooms have balconies and views over the harbor. Restaurants include the trendy Vong as well as international food. Conference facilities, translation service, indoor swimming pool, fitness center, beauty salon, and Cuban-style cigar divan. 541 rooms.

CAUSEWAY BAY/WAN CHAI

Century Hong Kong $$ *238 Jaffe Road, Tel. 2598 8888; Fax 2598 8866; <www.centuryhotels.com/century>.* This 23-story hotel is a short walk via covered walkway to the Convention and Exhibition Centre. Rooms are small, but equipped with double-paned windows to shut out traffic noise. Italian and Shanghainese restaurants. Business center, conference rooms, outdoor swimming pool, health center, and putting green. 517 rooms.

Empire Hotel $$ *33 Hennessy Road, Wan Chai; Tel. 2866 9111; Fax 2861 3121.* A good value in the heart of Wan Chai, it has many of the services and facilities of higher-priced hotels. Rooms are comfortable and pleasant with many amenities. Cantonese, a recommended Shanghainese restaurant, and a wine bar. Business and conference center, health center, swimming pool. 345 rooms.

The Excelsior $$$ *281 Gloucester Road, Causeway Bay; Tel. 2894 8888; Fax 2895 6459; <www.mandarin-oriental.com>.* This hotel is located near Victoria Park, and hosts many tour groups. Guest rooms are spacious, and have views over the bay or park. Cantonese and European restaurants and an English-style pub with live entertainment. Business center, rooftop tennis courts, fitness room, and Jacuzzi. 888 rooms.

Grand Hyatt Hong Kong $$$$ *1 Harbour Road, Wan Chai; Tel. 2588 1234; Fax 2802 0677.* A futuristic design of marble and glass, magnificent views over Hong Kong harbor, and an art-deco style interior characterize Hyatt International's Asian flagship hotel. It hosted President Clinton during his 1998 visit. Rooms are smart and contemporary with luxurious amenities. Eight restaurants, including Milanese and Cantonese cuisine, and JJ's, a hot nightspot. Business center, reference library, private boardroom, outdoor swimming pool, gym, tennis courts, golf driving range, jogging track. 570 rooms.

Park Lane $$$ *310 Gloucester Road, Causeway Bay; Tel. 2293 8888; Fax 2576 7853.* Across from Victoria Park, this attractive hotel with modern marble décor is near to restaurants, shops, and department stores. Room prices vary by floor. Top floor restaurant serves international cuisine with an Asian influence, and Stix is a bar/American restaurant/nightclub. Conference facilities and business center, health center, beauty salon. 792 rooms.

Renaissance Harbour View $$$ *1 Harbour Road, Wan Chai; Tel. 2802 8888; Fax 2802 8833; <www.renaissancehotels.com>.* This spectacular hotel adjoins the Convention and Exhibition Center on the Wan Chai waterfront. About half of the rooms have harbor views, and all are equipped with faxes and voice mail. The hotel's outdoor swimming pool is one of the largest in Hong Kong. Cantonese, Continental, and international restaurants. Business center and conference facilities, fitness center, beauty salon, rooftop tennis court, jogging track, garden, swimming pool, and nightclub. 862 rooms.

Wharney Hotel $$ *61-73 Lockhart Road, Wan Chai; Tel. 2861 1000; 2529 5133; e-mail <wharney@wlink.net>.* This pleasant hotel offers small but comfortable rooms; those with views are most expensive. Cantonese restaurant, Western/Asian buffet, bar with live entertainment. Business center, outdoor swimming pool and whirlpool, fitness center.

KOWLOON

Holiday Inn Golden Mile $$$ *50 Nathan Road, Tsim Sha Tsui; Tel. 2369 3111; Fax 2369 8016; <wwwgoldenmile.com>.* This hotel is conveniently located in the midst of Nathan Road's "Golden Mile" shopping. Rooms are good size and modern with floor-to-ceiling windows, although views are blocked by nearby buildings. Continental, Chinese, and Viennese restaurants. Business center, rooftop swimming pool, health center, and sauna. 600 rooms.

Grand Stanford Harbour View Hotel $$$ *70 Mody Road, Tsim Sha Tsui East; Tel. 2721 5161; Fax 2732 2233; <www.grandstanford.com>.* On the waterfront, with views over the harbor, this recently renovated hotel near the Coliseum has hosted the likes of David Bowie and Elton John. About half the rooms have harbor views. French, Italian, and Cantonese restaurants. Business center, heated outdoor pool, and gym. Free shuttle service in Tsim Sha Tsui. 580 rooms.

Imperial Hotel $ *30-34 Nathan Road, Tsim Sha Tsui; Tel. 2366 2201; Fax 2311 2360.* This simple hotel is conveniently located near the MTR station. The best rooms face Nathan Road, but can be noisy; ask for a room on a higher floor. Chinese and Italian restaurants and basement pub. 223 rooms.

Kowloon Hotel $$$ *19-21 Nathan Road, Tsim Sha Tsui; Tel. 2739 9811; Fax 369 8698.* A high-tech glass-and-steel hotel just behind the Peninsula and under the same management, this is an especially pleasant and convenient hotel for the business traveler. Rooms are small but attractive and cozy, and equipped with fax and computer with free internet access and e-mail. Cantonese and Italian restaurants, and Western/Asian buffet. Business center, beauty salon, and tour desk. 736 rooms.

Kowloon Shangri La $$$ *64 Mody Road, Tsim Sha Tsui; Tel. 2721 2111; Fax 2723 8686; <www.shangri-la.com>* A relaxed atmosphere and good service bring in repeat guests. Rooms are large and luxurious with dataports and all amenities; some have harbor views. Napa, on the 21st floor, offers California cuisine and a great view; there is also French, Cantonese and Japanese cuisine, Business center, small indoor swimming pool, health spa, and beauty salon. 725 rooms.

Majestic Hotel $ *348 Nathan Road, Yau Ma Tei; Tel. 2781 1773.* Located in a complex on upper Nathan Road, this hotel offers plain but comfortable, contemporary rooms. There is only a coffee shop, but the complex has shops, a cinema, and lots of restaurants. 393 rooms.

Marco Polo $$$ *Harbour City, 3 Canton Road, Tsim Sha Tsui; Tel. 2113 0888; Fax 2113 0022; <www.marcopolohotels.com>.* One of a trio of Marco Polo hotels, it's located in the Harbour City shopping complex, a step from the Star Ferry terminal; others are the higher-priced Hong Kong Hotel and the newly renovated Prince. It's a good choice for business travelers, with large desks and voice mail in all of its good-size rooms. One French restaurant, but Harbor City restaurants are nearby. Business center and conference facilities. 437 rooms.

Nathan Hotel $ *378 Nathan Road, Yau Ma Tei; Tel. 2388 5141; Fax 2770 4262; e-mail <nathanhk@hkstar.com>.* Recently renovated, this quiet and pleasant hotel near the Temple Street Night Market has spacious, nicely decorated no-frills rooms. The Penthouse restaurant serves Cantonese and Western food. Business center. 185 rooms.

Park Hotel $$ *61-65 Chatham Road South, Tsim Sha Tsui; Tel. 2366-1371; Fax 2739-7259; <www.parkhotel.com.hk>.* This is one of the best hotels in the moderate category, located across from the Science Museum. The lobby is attractive, and rooms are large and well-furnished. Western and Cantonese restaurants plus coffee and cake shop. Conference rooms and business services. 423 rooms.

Peninsula $$$$ *Salisbury Road, Tsim Sha Tsui; Tel. 2920 2888 ; Fax 2722 4170; <wwwpeninsula.com>.* Hong Kong's most historic hotel, first opened in 1928, is a study in colonial elegance. The famous English-style afternoon tea in the lobby is a must for visitors. Guest rooms in the new 32-story tower offer spectacular views; furnishings and amenities are sumptuous, and service is of the highest standard. Gaddi's is Hong Kong's premier French restaurant; other fine choices offer Pacific Rim, continental, Swiss, Japanese, and Cantonese cuisine. Business center, fax in all rooms, beauty salon, spa facilities, health club, swimming pool with sun terrace, music room. 300 rooms.

Regent $$$$ *18 Salisbury Road, Kowloon; Tel. 2721 1211; Fax 2739 4546; <wwwregenthotels.com>.* One of Hong Kong's top hotels, set on the waterfront, with luxurious granite and marble décor and harbor views. Guest rooms have spacious Italian marble bathrooms. Service is excellent, and the hotel has some of Hong Kong's best restaurants. Business center, outdoor swimming pool, health spa, exercise room. 602 rooms.

Royal Garden $$$ *69 Mody Road, Tsim Sha Tsui East; Tel. 2721 5215; Fax 2369 9976; <www.theroyalgardenhotel.com.hk>.* This is one of Hong Kong's most attractive hotels. All rooms open onto terraces overlooking a plant-filled 15-story atrium with pools and waterfalls. Rooms are cozy and inviting; the most expensive have harbor views. Italian, Cantonese, and Japanese restaurants and a restaurant in the atrium. Business center, rooftop swimming pool and Jacuzzi, sports center, beauty salon, fitness room, putting green. 422 rooms.

Royal Pacific Hotel and Towers $$-$$$ *33 Canton Road, Tsim Sha Tsui; Tel. 2736 1188; Fax 2736 1212; <www.royalpacific.com.hk>.* This is actually two hotels, located across from Kowloon Park and surrounded by greenery. The Royal Pacific is the more moderately priced. Its rooms are attractive but rather small. The Towers is more upscale, with harbor views from the highest rooms. The hotels share facilities. One restaurant, business center, fitness room, and squash courts. 673 rooms.

Salisbury YMCA **$** *41 Salisbury Road, Tsim Sha Tsui; Tel. 2268 7888; Fax 2739 9315; <www.ymcahk.org.hk>.* Reserve well in advance for this hotel, located next door to the Peninsula. It's one of the best bargains in Hong Kong, offering the facilities and service of much more expensive hotels. Rooms are simple in décor, but comfortable and well-equipped. Restaurant and food outlets. Two swimming pools, fitness gym, and sports center with squash courts and climbing wall. 380 units.

Shamrock **$** *223 Nathan Road, Yau Ma Tei; Kowloon; Tel. 2735 2271; Fax 2736 7354; <www.yp.com.hk/shamrock>.* In a rather plain modern building, the hotel has a lobby decorated with chandeliers and artwork. Guest rooms are rather small but clean (cheaper rooms are without windows). A restaurant serves Western food, and there's a bar and coffee shop. 148 rooms.

Sheraton Hong Kong Hotel and Towers **$$$$** *20 Nathan Road, Tsim Sha Tsui; Tel. 2369 1111; Fax 2739 8707; <www.sheraton.com/ hongkong>.* The hotel is near the harborfront, across from the Space Museum and the Art Museum. The décor is contemporary with Asian motifs. Guest rooms that face the harbor have great views. Restaurants include Japanese, an oyster bar, and a steak house, Morton's of Chicago. Business center and conference facilities, rooftop pool and Jacuzzi, sauna and gym, terrace gardens. 805 rooms.

NEW TERRITORIES

Regal Riverside **$$** *Tai Chung Kiu Road, Sha Tin; Tel. 2649 7878; Fax 2637 4748.* This large, modern hotel overlooks the Shing Mun River. Cantonese, Thai, and international restaurants. Business center and conference facilities, health club with full range of facilities, shuttle service to New Town Plaza and Tsim Sha Tsui. 789 rooms.

Royal Park **$$** *8 Pak Hok Ting Street, Sha Tin; Tel. 2601 2111; Fax 2601 3666.* This hotel near the Sha Tin Racecourse and New Town Plaza is easily accessed from the city. Chiu Chow and Japanese restaurants, coffee shop, squash, tennis and jogging facilities, swimming pool, health center, business center, and conference facilities. Special facilities for guests with disabilities. 436 rooms.

MACAU

Lisboa $$ *Av. de Lisboa, No. 2-4, Macau; Tel. (853)577666 Fax 567193; <www.macau.ctm.net/Lisboa>.* This huge hotel on the waterfront with its cylindrical tower can't be missed. It has every facility, including casinos, a nightclub, and show entertainment. Chinese, Portuguese, Continental, and Asian restaurants. Conference and secretarial services, children's center, outdoor swimming pool, fitness center, and free shuttle bus service. 1,000 rooms.

Posada de São Tiago $$$ *Fortaleza de S. Tiago da Barrra, Av. da República; Tel. (853)378111; Fax 552170.* This charming small inn is built around the ruins of a fort dating from 1629. Guests here are treated with true Portuguese hospitality. Rooms are in Portuguese style with furniture imported from Portugal and blue-glazed tile; most have balconies. Macanese cuisine at Os Gatos, classic Portuguese cuisine at Café Da Barra. Outdoor swimming pool. 23 rooms.

GUANGZHOU (CANTON)

Garden Hotel $$ *368 Huanshi Dong Lu; Tel. (020)8333 8989; Fax 8335 0467; <www.gardenhotel-guangzhou.com>.* This hotel is well-named for its beautiful gardens. It is located in upscale northern Guangzhou, and has a spectacular lobby with a huge unsupported ceiling. Standard rooms have all amenities but a somewhat plain décor. Restaurants offer Western and Asian cuisine. Business services, swimming pool, tennis court, health club, and dance club. 1,112 rooms.

White Swan $$$ *1 South Shamian Street; Tel. (020)8188 6968; Fax 8186 1188.* This luxury hotel is sited on historic Shamian Island beside the Pearl River. A spectacular décor includes a lobby with a cascading waterfall, and rooms are furnished with reproduction Chinese antiques. Nine restaurants. Business services, two swimming pools, health club, driving range, tennis courts, dance club, and cruises on the Pearl River. 843 rooms.

Recommended Restaurants

Dining is one of the great Hong Kong experiences. The city is crammed with all kinds of restaurants, specializing in every imaginable kind of cuisine. Kowloon has a particularly high concentration of restaurants. It is impossible to choose more than a few from the vast range of possibilities.

As everywhere else, the restaurant scene is in a constant state of flux, so it's wise to call and make a reservation before you leave your hotel.

The price symbols below are intended as a guide only, and are based on a standard three-course meal (or Asian equivalent), in Hong Kong dollars. These prices do not cover alcoholic drinks or such notoriously expensive items as bird's nest or shark's fin.

$$$$	over HK$600 per person
$$$	HK$300 to HK$600 per person
$$	HK$150 to HK$300 per person
$	below HK$150 per person

KOWLOON

City Chiu Chow Restaurant $$ *1/F, East Ocean Centre, 98 Granville Road, Tsim Sha Tsui; Tel. 2723 6226.* Open Monday to Thursday 11am to 3pm and 5pm to midnight, Friday to Sunday 11am to midnight. This large, bright restaurant overlooking a garden serves hearty Chiu Chow dishes and a variety of regional specialties. It features a big fish tank, and the shark's fin soup is more strongly flavored than the Cantonese variety.

Felix $$$$ *The Peninsula, Salisbury Road; Tel. 2920 2888, Ext. 3188.* Open daily 6pm to 2am. This restaurant is not to be missed: the marvelous view and the striking Phillipe Stark design are nearly as important as the food. The Pacific Rim fusion cuisine is delectable.

Golden Island Bird's Nest Chiu Chow Restaurant $$ *3/F-4/F, BCC Building, 25-31 Carnarvon Road, Tsim Sha Tsui; Tel. 2369 5211.* Open daily 11am to 3pm and 5:30 to 11:30pm. The specialty here is the bird's nest dishes, expensive but less than elsewhere. It's right next to the Star Ferry Terminal. The cuisine is low-cholesterol, a good choice for the health-conscious.

Great Shanghai $$ *26 Prat Avenue, Tsim Sha Tsui; Tel. 2366 8158.* Open daily 11am to 2:30pm and 6:30 to 11pm. Well-established restaurant serving good-value Shanghainese dishes. Beggar's chicken is the house specialty (call in your order ahead). Typical warming dishes are Shanghainese dumplings, eel and bean curd dishes, and cabbage stews. Shanghainese wines are also available. Friendly and helpful service.

Heichinrou Restaurant $$$ *2/F, Lippo Sun Plaza, 28 Canton Road, Tsimshatsui; Tel. 2375 7123.* A chic Cantonese restaurant with stark modern décor. A good place for dim sum. Specialties include roasted pigeon with Chinese cheese sauce. There's a branch at the Times Square Shopping Center in Causeway Bay.

Jade Garden Restaurant $$ *BCC Bank Building, 25-31 Carnarvon Road, Tsim Sha Tsui; Tel. 2369 8311.* Open daily 7:30am to midnight. Classic dishes, dim sum, and seasonal specialties. Ask for the recommended dishes of the day. Other branches are at Star House, 3 Salisbury Road, Tsim Sha Tsui; and Jardine House at 1 Connaught Place in Central.

Jimmy's Kitchen $$ *Kowloon Centre, 29 Ashley Road, Tsim Sha Tsui; Tel. 2376 0327.* Open daily 11:30am to midnight. One of Hong Kong's oldest restaurants, Jimmy's specializes in British food, but also has curries and other Asian dishes. There's also a Jimmy's in the South China Building, 1-3 Wyndham Street in Central.

Joyful Vegetarian $$ *530 Nathan Road, Yau Ma Tei; Tel. 2780 2230.* Open 11am to 11pm. It is hard to find strictly vegetarian food in Hong Kong; most chefs add meat broth to vegetarian dishes. This restaurant is one of a handful that specializes in true vegetarian meals. Try the delicious country-style hotpot.

Lai Ching Heen $$$$ *Regent Hotel, 18 Salisbury Road, Tsim Sha Tsui; Tel. 2721 1211.* Elegant restaurant with opulent décor and views over the harbor, serves exquisite and innovative Cantonese and Chinese food. The menu changes each lunar month.

Pizzeria $$ *2/F Kowloon Hotel, 19-21 Nathan Road, Tsim Sha Tsui; Tel. 2929 2888.* Open daily noon to 3pm and 6 to 11pm. Despite its name, this restaurant specializes in pasta, with a menu that changes often. The atmosphere is relaxed, and there's a wide range of choices. Eight kinds of pizza are also served.

Salisbury $ *Salisbury YMCA, 4/F, 41 Salisbury Road, Tsim Sha Tsui; Tel. 2369 2211, ext. 1026.* Open Monday to Saturday noon to 2:30pm, daily 6:30 to 9:30pm. One of the best places for an inexpensive meal, the dining room offers generous lunch and dinner buffets of Asian and Western food. There is also an à la carte menu of sandwiches and pasta.

Spice Market $$ *3/F, Marco Polo Prince, 23 Canton Road, Tsim Sha Tsui; Tel. 2113 6046.* Open daily noon to 2:30pm and 6:30 to 10pm. This pleasant restaurant specializes in a wide variety of Asian foods: Japanese, Chinese, Thai, Indian curries, hotpots, satays, and more.

Tai Woo Restaurant $ *14-16 Hillwood Road, Tsim Sha Tsui; Tel. 2368 5420.* Open until 3am. Popular favorites include seafood dishes such as steamed garoupa or sautéed scallops. The set meals are a good way of sampling a range of Cantonese dishes.

CENTRAL

Ashoka Restaurant $ *G/F, 57-59 Wyndham Street; Tel. 2524 9623.* Open daily noon to 2:30pm and 6 to 10:30pm. Elegant Indian restaurant serving delicately spiced northern Indian cuisine. The wide range of dishes offered includes Tandoori, curries, and vegetarian specialties. The place is small, so there may be a wait.

Beirut $$ *G/F-1/F, 27 D'Aguilar Street, Lan Kwai Fong, Central; Tel. 2804 6611.* Open Monday to Saturday noon to midnight, Sunday 4 to 11pm. This restaurant offers an extensive menu of Lebanese specialties, including *shawarma* and *lahme bil agine* (a kind of Lebanese pizza). The homemade hummus is the best in Hong Kong. Ideal for lunch.

Blue $$$ *45 Lyndhurst Terrace, Central; Tel. 2815 4005.* Open for lunch and dinner. This chic and trendy restaurant at the junction with Hollywood Road has a minimalist décor and imaginative Pacific Rim food. Reservations are advised.

Benkay Japanese Restaurant $$$ *1st Basement, Gloucester Tower, The Landmark; Des Voeux Road Central; Tel. 2521 3344.* Traditional pine-paneled restaurant serving teppanyaki and sushi delicacies, kaiseki, or sukiyaki or shabu-shabu set meals. The à la carte menu features Kyoto-style cuisine; grilled codfish and eel are particularly recommended.

California $$ *G/F, Grand Progress Building, 15 Lan Kwai Fong; Tel. 2521 1345.* Open daily noon to 2:30pm and 6 to 11pm, to midnight weekends. Chic American-style restaurant and bar popular with the after-work crowd from Central. Chef Jason Hyatt offers such dishes as marinated grilled beef salad with pickled ginger, aioli, and arugula pesto.

Luk Yu Tea House $$$ *24-26 Stanley Street; Tel. 2523 5464.* Open 7am to 10pm. This place has been around for 60 years, and is a living piece of colonial history with its carved wooden doors and paneling. It is a popular venue for excellent dim sum. No credit cards.

Peking Garden $$ *Shop 003, The Mall, Pacific Place, 88 Queensway; Tel. 2845 8452.* Open daily 11:30am to 3pm and 5:30 to midnight. Lively restaurant specializing in northern Chinese dishes. Watch fresh noodles being made each evening, and enjoy the Peking duck-carving exhibitions and beggar's chicken clay-breaking ceremonies. Other branches are at Star

House, 3 Salisbury Road in Tsim Sha Tsui and at 500 Hennessy Road, Causeway Bay.

Vong $$$$ *Mandarin Oriental Hotel, 5 Connaught Road; Tel. 2825 4028.* Open daily noon to 3pm and 6pm to midnight. A dramatic restaurant with a creative crossover cuisine of Asian flavors and French techniques. There are extensive vegetarian offerings. The tasting menu is recommended.

THE PEAK

Café Deco $$$ *1/F-2/F Peak Galleria, 118 Peak Road; Tel. 2849 5111.* Open daily 10am to midnight. You won't find the greatest food here, but it has one of the best views in the city. There's a variety of Asian and Continental dishes, an oyster bar, and live jazz on the weekends.

Peak Café $$ *121 Peak Road; Tel. 2849 7868.* Open 10:30am to midnight. This café has become a Hong Kong institution. In a 19th-century building at the top of Victoria Peak, it has old-world charm and stunning views over the south side of the island as well as excellent Asian food with some Western dishes. Ideal for lunch or tea after a ride up on the tram from Central.

WAN CHAI

American Restaurant $ *Golden Star Building G/F-2/F, 20 Lockhart Road; Tel. 2527 1000.* Open daily 11am to 11:30pm. Popular Peking restaurant (despite the name), featuring northern Chinese dishes, such as seafood noodles and the classic Peking duck. Specialty is a "Four Great Happiness" combination dish of pork, beef, prawns, and chicken.

Can Do Restaurant $ *1/F, 78 Johnston Road. Tel. 2527 7868.* Specialties include sweet-and-sour won ton and special congees. Serves good-value snacks and meals, and service is friendly. A popular restaurant with both visitors and locals.

Cinta Restaurant $$ *1/F-2/F, Shing Yip Building, 10 Fenwick Street; Tel. 2527 1199.* Open daily 11am to 3pm and 6pm to 2am. A friendly restaurant serving Indonesian favorites such as satay, prawn chili, fried squid, and beef Rendang. Filipino dishes include crispy pata (pork leg) and mixed adobo. There are also Malaysian favorites. Live music nightly.

Fook Lam Moon $$$$ *35-45 Johnston Road; Tel. 2866 0663.* Open daily 11:30am to 3pm and 6:30 to 11:30pm. One of the top Cantonese restaurants in the city. Seafood is the specialty, and here you can try shark's fin soup. There is also a branch at Luna Court in Tsim Sha Tsui.

Viceroy $$ *2/F, Sun Hung Kai Centre, 30 Harbour Road; Tel. 2827 7777.* Open daily noon to 3pm and 6 to 11pm. Indian restaurant with panoramic harbor views from an outdoor terrace, serving subtly flavored Tandoori, curry, and vegetarian specialties, and an all-you-can-eat weekday buffet feast.

CAUSEWAY BAY

Cammino Restaurant $$ *l/F, The Excelsior, 281 Gloucester Road, Causeway Bay; Tel. 2837 6780.* New chef, Michele Rhodelli brings his fine Italian cusine to Hong Kong with an appetizing menu of classic and modern Italian dishes. Try octopus with shaved grana and white truffle, or veal with peppers and mozzarella in zucchini and *vin santo* sauce.

Kung Lak Tam $ *Lok Sing Centre, 31 Yee Wo Street; Tel. 2890 3127.* Open daily 11am to 11pm. This Shanghainese vegetarian restaurant uses only the freshest produce, no MSG. The vegetable soup and fried noodles are especially delectable.

Red Pepper $$$ *7 Lan Fong Road; Tel. 2577 3811.* Open daily 11:30am to 11:15pm. The right place for those who like spicy food. Szechwan-style cuisine in a friendly, relaxed atmosphere. The staff will help you to order a meal that suits your taste.

Forever Green $$ *93-95 Leighton Road; Tel. 2890 3448.* Open daily noon to 3pm and 6pm to 5am. A great place for Korean/Taiwanese food. A menu with pictures helps out the novice. Noodle dishes are good value.

ABERDEEN

Aberdeen Tai Pak Floating Restaurant $$-$$$ *Aberdeen Harbour; Tel. 2553 9111*. Open Sunday to Thursday 11:30am to 9:30pm, Friday and Saturday 11:30am to 11:30pm. Hong Kong's huge floating restaurants with their fantastic decoration have long been a tourist attraction. The Tai Pak has undergone a recent renovation. It has added a buffet of Asian dishes to its seafood specialties, and offers a free sampan ride through the typhoon shelter.

MACAU

Military Club $$$ *Av. da Praia Grande, 795; Tel. 714009*. Open daily noon to 3pm and 7 to 11pm. The atmospheric dining hall of the 1870 Clube Militar de Macau, with its high ceilings and arched windows is a rare glimpse into the past. The extensive menu offers excellent Portuguese cuisine.

Fat Siu Lau $$ *Rua da Felicidade, 64; Tel. 573580*. Open daily 11:30am to 11:30pm. Macau's oldest restaurant has been renovated in a modern art-deco style. The Macanese menu includes a traditional roast pigeon prepared according to a 90-year-old recipe. No credit cards.

O Porto Interior $$ *Rua do Almirante Sergio, 259B; Tel. 967770*. Open daily noon to 3pm and 6 to 11:30pm. Located on the Inner Harbour and not far from the Maritime Museum, this restaurant is notable for its colonnaded façade and its walls covered with azulejos and carved wooden grilles. The carefully prepared Macanese dishes are an excellent value.

GUANGZHOU (CANTON)

Lian Xiang Lou $$ *67 Dishifu Lu; Tel. 8139 1191*. This outstanding restaurant is located on an interesting older shopping street that has survived in Guangzhou's relentless new construction. The décor is elaborate and elegant, and the Cantonese dishes are simply delicious.

INDEX